**WALKER
BOOKS**

First published 2021 by Walker Books Ltd
87 Vauxhall Walk, London SE11 5HJ

4 6 8 10 9 7 5

Text © 2021 Seth Burkett and Matt Oldfield
Interior illustrations © 2021 Tom Jennings
Cover illustrations © 2021 Dan Leydon

The right of Seth Burkett and Matt Oldfield to be identified
as authors and of Dan Leydon and Tom Jennings to be
identified respectively as cover illustrator and inside
illustrator of this work has been asserted in accordance with
the Copyright, Designs and Patents Act 1988.

This book has been typeset in Agenda, Barmeno,
Intro Black, ITC Machine and Bodoni.

Printed and bound in UK

British Library Cataloguing in Publication Data: a catalogue
record for this book is available from the British Library

ISBN 978-1-5295-0029-5

www.walker.co.uk

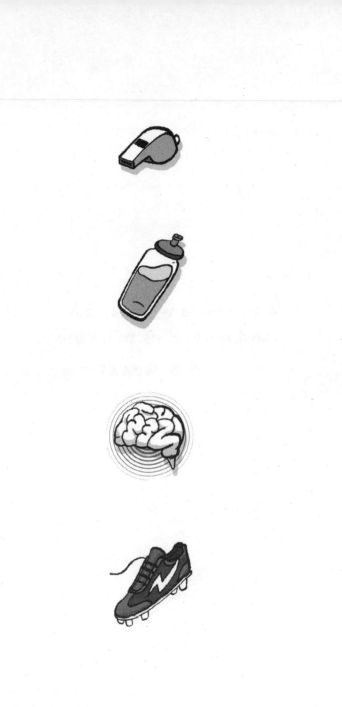

To all those who believed in us
and helped us to be better.

S.B. & M.O.

# PLAY LiKE YOUR
# F⚽OTBALL HEROES

### PRO TIPS
### FOR BECOMING
### A TOP
### PLAYER

# SETH BURKETT ⚽ MATT OLDFIELD

# CONTENTS

## TRAIN SMART — 15

## THINK SMART — 79

# LIVE SMART 135

# PLAY SMART 193

# STRIKING OUT

If you're reading these words, hello and well done! This book is going to change your football life. (Hopefully!)

Yes, whether you're just kicking off your passion or you've been playing the game for years, we've got you covered. With tons of top tips and stories from football's superstars we will help you to become the best player you can be.

"OK, that sounds extremely exciting, but how are words on a page going to help me improve my performances on the pitch?" We know that's what you're wondering! (Warning: we read minds, as well as books about football.)

Well, this is no ordinary guide to the beautiful game – oh no, we'll be going way beyond the basic skills. To become a top footballer, you'll need a lot more than just talent. Yes, fancy footwork helps, but really you play the game with your whole body, and especially your brain. It takes dedication, determination, discipline and teamwork, and – as you're about to find out – you can learn all that from your heroes too:

- American playmaker **Christian Pulisic** is known for his deadly dribbling and clever passing, but how did a robot football machine prepare him for greatness?

- When we think of **Mo Salah**, the "Egyptian King", we think of super speed and a lethal left foot, but how did learning from disappointments lead him to become an even better player?
- Argentinian striker **Sergio Agüero** is one of the greatest goal-scorers in the world, but what can he teach us about rest and recovery?
- We know England star **Lucy Bronze** can do it all on the football pitch, so what has made her such an amazing all-round player?

But before we give away all our secrets straight away, let's tell you a bit more about how this book works. People like to talk about football being "a game of two halves", but we're going to flout the rules with this book. Instead, we're breaking the beautiful game down into *dun dun duuuuuuun* *four quarters* instead.

Right now, you're probably thinking, "What?! Are you guys crazy?" but we're not, we promise. (Well, only crazy about football.) You see, in order to help you become the best player you can be, we're going to need more than just two categories. In order to become the next **Megan Rapinoe** or **Jadon Sancho**, and play like your football heroes, you're going to have to:

## 1. TRAIN SMART

You know that you need to work hard to reach the top, but what should you practise, and when?

## 2. THINK SMART

Things might not always go your way on the football field, so what can you do to stay focused on achieving your dreams?

## 3. LIVE SMART

Everyone's always telling you to stay fit and healthy, but what does that really mean?

## 4. PLAY SMART

How can you take everything you learn on the training ground and transfer it to the big pitch to make every game a ten out of ten?

In each section, we're going to show you why and how you can become a hero, using stories about your favourite players and information that we've learned from the worlds of football and science. And just in case you don't believe us (or the smart scientists), we'll also be giving you the inside scoop on four of your favourite superstars, as well as challenges for you to tackle and quizzes for you to test yourself.

So, sounds like the best book you've ever heard of, right? Great, but before we kick off this adventure into the world of football's heroes, we should really introduce ourselves.

01 SETH BURKETT

This is Seth. He supports Peterborough United (who?) and his favourite player is **Ronaldinho**. As well as being an author, Seth is also a former professional footballer for clubs in Brazil and Sri Lanka. Despite Seth's much superior football talent, he is happy to work with Matt because they are friends – even after all the hours they've spent arguing over which heroes to write about in this book.

But what about X?

No, Y is so much better!

You smell!

No, you do!

I don't want to write this book with you any more!

Fine!

Actually, I've changed my mind – let's keep Y but can we have Z too?

And this is Matt. He supports Southampton and his favourite player is **James Ward-Prowse**. Before he started writing this book with Seth, Matt was pretty bad at football, but now he's so good that he's just received an England call-up. Only joking – he's still pretty bad at football. Thankfully, Matt is a lot better at writing about the beautiful game than he is at playing it.

02 MATT OLDFIELD

Off the pitch, Seth and Matt
make a great writing team.
Actually, you can be the judge
of that for yourself.

OK, that's enough from us – it's time for you to get started
on your quest for total football knowledge. First stop:
the training ground.

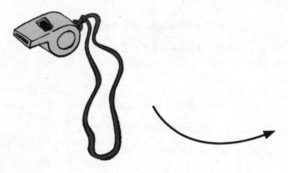

# PRACTICE MAKES...

Did you know that NOBODY is born great? When we watch our football heroes play, it may seem that their passes are superhuman, that their shots are more powerful than a charging elephant and that their skills come from another planet. But there is one simple way that all of those amazing players became amazing footballers, and that's ...

**[Drum roll, please.]**

... hard work! A *lot* of hard work, actually.

OK, you can stop drumming now.

Let's start with a really cool fact. Right now, you are better at football than Argentinian superstar **Lionel Messi** was at one point in his life. That seems ridiculous, right? Messi is so good that he could nutmeg a mermaid. He could score a hat-trick while blindfolded. He could do a million keepy-uppies with an orange.

But here's the thing, Messi couldn't do millions of keepy-uppies in his cot. He couldn't dribble a ball before he could walk. Once he was on his feet, though, Messi started to learn new skills. He played for thousands and thousands of hours and worked so hard that he became the best in the world – maybe ever!

Wouldn't it be amazing if someone could tell you exactly how much hard work is needed to become as brilliant as Messi? Well, your luck is in. They have!

Back in 1993, Karl Anders Ericsson and a group of brainy academics studied how young violin students practised. In their scientific paper – called "The Role of Deliberate Practice in the Acquisition of Expert Performance" – they revealed that, on average, expert musicians practised for a total of 10,000 hours over ten years.

You may not have 10,000 hours that you can spend training. But what you do have is a chance to use the time that you have constructively. If you want to become a world-class footballer, you can't just practise the bits you really enjoy, such as shooting or mad tekkers. Even Messi, who loves nothing more than dribbling round millions of defenders, practises far more than just that skill. He spends plenty of time working on the parts of his game that he finds less exciting. Just like Messi, you need to use your practice time very carefully if you want to improve.

That's why we are here to help you! In this section, we're going to show you how to make the most of however many hours you can spare by training smart like your football heroes.

You'll learn to:

**become a ball master**

**follow the feedback loop**

**practise with purpose**

**show off your transferable skills**

Ready? Last one out on the pitch has to run five laps!

A skill is having the ability to do something well. But in football you need more than one skill. In fact, you need loads of them! A game is played between twenty-two people in lots of different positions. Each position has its own demands. A goalkeeper needs a different set of skills from a midfielder. A defender needs a different set of skills from a striker. Even a full-back needs a different set of skills from a centre-back.

This means that when you train, you have to focus on more than just one skill. It's no good being awesome at passing if you can't first control the ball. So what skills are we talking about?

## BECOME A HERO ↵

Think of your favourite footballer in the whole entire world. Grab a piece of paper and write down all of the skills that make that player amazing. OK, now compare your list to our suggestions on the next page.

When we were thinking about skills, six-time Ballon d'Or winner **Lionel Messi** came to mind. With more than 500 career goals and thirty-four top trophies, he's got skills so magical that even the world's best defenders end up flat on their faces in the presence of his greatness (sorry, **Jérôme Boateng**!). These are some of the main technical skills that Messi needs when he plays football:

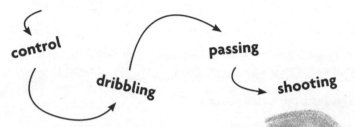

control

dribbling

passing

shooting

These skills require you to move your body to bring about an action. Learning different techniques is all about how you move your body.

All of these skills above can be summed up as ball mastery. Sounds kind of cool, right? Like a football wizard.

But how can you become an ultimate ball master like Messi?

# TRAIN WITH VARIETY

This won't come as a surprise, but to become good at a skill you have to actually do it. A lot. We're talking 10,000 hours, remember? Fortunately, there are loads of different ways to learn skills. But no matter how you learn, it's important to practise that skill in a variety of conditions.

When we say "conditions", we don't mean rain, wind and snow (although pros do keep practising, no matter the weather!). No, we're talking about **constant, variable** and **random conditions**.

Confused? Don't worry, we're about to explain. Let's use the skill of control as an example and start with...

## CONSTANT CONDITIONS

This is any practice you do where the conditions don't change. So, no team-mates and no opponents – it's just you and the ball. Constant training is really useful for learning basic techniques. A super simple – and constant – way to improve your control is to practise against a wall, where you know the ball will bounce back in a predictable way.

23

That's how so many football superstars started out, including Messi. Growing up in Rosario, Argentina, he was mostly a quiet, well-behaved boy, but there was one thing that got him into trouble with his neighbours. What did one of them say? "He used to interrupt my siesta [that's an afternoon nap] – all the time kicking a football against my wall."

It's incredibly important to use both your strong foot and your weak foot equally in every training session. If you don't, you'll only be half as good at football. Some people say that Messi "only has one foot" (his left), but here's a stat for you: he's still scored 13% of his goals with his right. If you also feel comfortable playing with either foot, that will help you to be twice as good as footballers who only use their strong foot. It's a bit like a superpower, because defenders have no idea which way you're going to go as you dribble towards goal.

So, our message to you is: be more Messi (although choose your wall carefully, especially if you have grumpy neighbours!).

# BECOME A HERO ↴

Throw the ball against a wall and then try to control it when it rebounds. The idea is that the ball should land just in front of your foot as you control it so you can immediately make a pass. Use different parts of each foot to practise your control. Try the instep, outside, sole and laces. If you're feeling really adventurous, you can even use your heel (this is so tricky that it's basically Ball Mastery Level 1,000,000). First use your right foot to control the ball, then the next time, control it with your left foot.

Once you feel comfortable practising your control in constant conditions, the next step is to try it in...

## VARIABLE CONDITIONS

This is training which aims to get you used to performing a skill in different situations, such as receiving passes that have unpredictable outcomes. Perhaps they soar straight at your knee or bobble along the ground, for example. So instead of a wall, try asking a friend to practise with you.

## BECOME A HERO

Try the same challenge as before but ask your friend to pass the ball to you. Their passes will come at different heights and angles and speeds (especially if your football friend has a foot like a rocket launcher), meaning you'll need to control the ball in different ways. To make it even harder, you could ask another friend to defend from behind and add some extra pressure.

Training by yourself is great, but training with friends and family is way more fun. During his early footballing days, Messi often practised his skills with (and against) his brothers, Rodrigo and Matías, and his cousins, **Maxi** and **Emanuel Biancucchi**. His cousins both became professional footballers too, playing for teams in South America, so those family battles must have been epic!

Right, back to you – now that you've worked on your control with a friend, you're ready to test yourself in...

## RANDOM CONDITIONS

Every football game is played in random conditions. Players move into random positions, the ball comes to you in a variety of ways, teams use different tactics: you can never predict exactly what is going to happen!

This is what random training prepares you for. To practise control in random conditions, you need a defender who tries to win the ball from you. An example of this is a game called rondo, which every elite football team plays (often as a warm-up). It's basically a fancy name for piggy/monkey-in-the-middle.

Messi was already a rondo champion from his childhood playing for Newell's Old Boys in Argentina, but he became a rondo black belt when he moved to Barcelona at the age of thirteen. The game is a key part of training at the club's academy, La Masia, because it helps teach the young footballers the awesome close control they need to play the "Barcelona Way" (or *tiki-taka* if you speak Spanish/Football).

## BECOME A HERO ↴

Form a circle of four or more players, with another one or two players in the middle (we'd recommend four versus one, or five versus two). The aim of the game is to keep possession of the ball by passing it around, while avoiding the piggies/monkeys in the middle. Sounds easy? Wait until you give it a go!

In rondo, the ball comes to you at random and you can't predict how the defenders are going to move. You learn which control is best in which situation. Is it a big touch out in front of your feet so you can easily play the next pass, or is it a touch to stop the ball dead so that you can then shield it from the defender? Best learn quickly, because if you lose control of the ball, you have to take your turn in the middle!

To get better at any football skill and become a ball master like Messi, it's best to practise in each of these three conditions. If you only ever tried constant training, you wouldn't learn how to control the ball under the pressure of a defender. And if you went straight to the random world of rondo, you'd find it harder to learn the basics. Eventually, you'll get the hang of each condition. And once you find out what works for you, you'll be able to take the next step towards using your magic wands (your two feet) to become a football wizard like Messi!

When you start to learn a new skill, it can be frustrating. The ball bounces in funny ways and doesn't do what you want it to. You've watched your favourite players perform the skill and you try to copy it exactly the same way, but it just doesn't work the way it should.

But fear not!

It takes time to learn a skill. If it was easy to master a skill, then everyone would be as good as **Ada Hegerberg**, the superstar striker, who in 2018 became the first-ever winner of the Women's Ballon d'Or.

As Ada's story will show, learning a new skill takes commitment and persistence. So, when you miscontrol the ball for the millionth time or dribble into the cone once again or whatever it may be, it doesn't mean you're bad at those skills. It just means you haven't found the right way yet.

But trust us: you will.

# THE FEEDBACK LOOP

The good news is that there is no single right way to perform a football skill. If one method isn't working for you, try to find one that does. This is called trial and error.

Take shooting, for example. How did Hegerberg get so good at it? Well, as a kid growing up in Norway, she played a lot of football and spent a lot of time practising. When she wasn't taking on the local boys and girls, she was often out on the pitch with her sister, **Andrine**, taking shot after shot against their dad, Stein Erik. Sometimes Hegerberg scored, and sometimes she didn't, but by trying out different shooting methods she was able to discover which finishes worked best for her:

**Is it low and hard into the bottom corner?**

**How about the long-range curler into the top corner?**

**Or maybe even the cheeky chip over the keeper?**

Alongside her own trial-and-error experiments, Hegerberg also did lots of extra analysis work with her dad. "We have been training together since I was nine – he knows me, he watches a lot of my games. It's always about picking out details in order to stay sharp, season after season."

Together, the Hegerbergs looked at what Ada did well and worked on areas where she could still improve. Each time she tried a different type of shot, they looked at the result, and then assessed what she needed to change. This is called the **feedback loop**.

try skill → see the result → analyse → make a change →

FEEDBACK

After each shot, Hegerberg would ask herself all kinds of questions as to how she could improve the technique the next time. Even if it was a weak shot that trickled along the grass or a mishit that flew into the trees, Ada never gave up or stormed off the pitch in a huff. Instead, she questioned her game and learned to challenge herself.

**Is this training method working?**

**Why am I finding it hard?**

**Did I move my leg too quickly?**

**Was my standing foot in the correct position?**

**Am I connecting with the ball in the right place?**

**Do I need to lean back more?**

**What about my follow-through?**

After asking those questions and talking things through with her father, Ada always made changes. She tried a new technique where she connected with the ball slightly lower or brought her leg forward more powerfully to give a strong follow-through. When those changes proved more successful, she asked herself the same questions again.

The feedback loop worked wonders for Hegerberg. The more she practised her shooting, the more she perfected the skill, and the more goals she scored:

First, twelve in twenty-four games for her local club Kolbotn

Then a phenomenal fifty-four in thirty-five for the French and European champions, Lyon!

Followed by thirty-three in twenty-six for Stabæk

If you want to see confident finishing at its finest, watch the highlights of Hegerberg's hat-trick in the 2019 Champions League final against Barcelona:

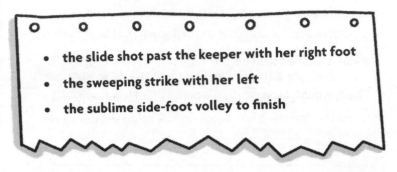

- **the slide shot past the keeper with her right foot**
- **the sweeping strike with her left**
- **the sublime side-foot volley to finish**

That, right there, is a striker who has worked out the best ways to score!

And despite all of Ada's success, she's still learning from the feedback loop. After all, a true superstar is never satisfied. During the summer breaks, she often returns home for more coaching sessions with her father and Andrine, who plays for the Italian club, Roma. What an amazing football family!

## IT'S ALL ABOUT YOU

When you use a feedback loop, you eventually discover the best way to perform the skill. Remember, it's what is right for YOU.

# BECOME A HERO ↴

OK, it's your turn to learn from the feedback loop. Pick a particular skill that you want to work on and try three different ways to perform it. See which works best for you, then see if there's anything you can do to improve it. Make a change, then try again.

This is our example for improving your shooting.

| Shooting technique | Inspiration | Change 1 | Change 2 | Change 3 |
|---|---|---|---|---|
| Curler | Steph Houghton | Run up from the side | Try the inside and outside of the foot | Stop the follow-through halfway |
| Knuckleball | Cristiano Ronaldo | Increase/decrease length of run-up | Use the instep | Pull the striking leg higher on the follow-through |
| Power kick | Ada Hegerberg | Use the laces | Strike in the middle of the ball instead of the bottom | Lean forward when hitting the ball |

There are lots of people who could help you with your feedback loop. Your friends, family and team-mates can give you pointers. Your coaches are well placed to help analyse your technique and suggest changes.

Watching your hero perform the skill with success is another great way to learn. See the movements they make and how they perform the skill, then try to copy them. If you've got a video camera or smartphone, you can even film yourself and see how you compare!

So you see: the more that you try a skill, then develop it through training, the more naturally the movements will come to you. At first, you will have to think about where to position your foot, how hard to cushion the ball and the best way to balance – even once you have the technique that works for you. Soon enough, though, these movements will become second nature. You'll position your foot in the right place, strike the ball in the ideal place without thinking and see the net ripple. That's the beauty of the feedback loop. The more you practise, the better you'll get. Especially when you practise with purpose.

# 03 TRAIN LIKE PULISIC
## PRACTISE WITH PURPOSE

# CHRISTIAN PULISIC

**NATIONALITY:** American

**POSITION:** Attacking Midfielder

**HERO MOMENT:** winning the German Cup in 2017 with Borussia Dortmund

Now, it's time to take you on a football study trip. Make sure you're strapped in comfortably for the ride. The next stop is Germany. Dortmund, to be precise.

All of the top footballers learned their skills with the help of football coaches. And the football coaches at top German club Borussia Dortmund have helped to develop some of the world's best footballers, such as **Marco Reus**, **Antonio Rüdiger**, plus American superstars **Giovanni Reyna** and **Christian Pulisic**. To help their players train smart, the coaches at Dortmund use the latest technology and, in particular, a special robot machine called a **Footbonaut**. Sounds cool, right? It costs around £2.5 million and it looks a bit like this:

Players train individually in the Footbonaut. Inside, there's a cage with seventy-two gates cut into the walls. In the middle is a circle, where the player stands. When the player is ready, the machine fires a ball into the circle. The ball can come from anywhere, at any speed and any height, so the player must look around constantly. Once the ball has been controlled, they must turn and pass it into whichever one of the seventy-two gates lights up.

How fun does that sound? It's like a football version of whack-a-mole!

The Footbonaut is a great example of the variable training that we talked about earlier in this section. Sometimes coaches even add a defender to make it really hard for the person training (any miscontrol will be snaffled up by the defender). The coaches record each player's score and then track how quickly they develop.

# TIME FOR A CHALLENGE

For some, the improvement is incredible. Take Pulisic, for example. He was fifteen years old when he made the big move from the USA to Germany. As soon as he arrived, he saw that he had some serious catching-up to do – at Dortmund, even the Under-9s get to train in the

Footbonaut! So, for his first few years at the club, Pulisic pretty much lived there, battling the machine every day and boosting his ball control, his awareness and his passing accuracy.

Six years later, thanks to all those hours practising in the cage, Pulisic now has one of the best first touches in the game, and he uses it to turn quickly and attack. Once he gets on the ball, he always seems to know what to do next, whether that's pass, dribble or shoot. That's why Chelsea paid £58 million to sign him in 2019.

OK, so it worked for Pulisic, but what makes the Footbonaut such a powerful training machine?

It gives the player lots of touches of the ball. The Dortmund coaches know that every time you touch the ball, you get better. Just fifteen minutes in the Footbonaut gives young Dortmund players as many touches as they would get in a week of regular training (around 5,000 touches, in case you were wondering!).

The training happens at high speed. By making the training session faster than a match, it means that performing the same skills in a match will seem easier. Train fast to train smart.

The Footbonaut is fun. When training is enjoyable, you're more motivated to keep on training. You won't want to train for 10,000 hours if training is boring – you will if it's fun!

It gives instant feedback. If you are unable to control the ball in the circle or your pass misses one of the gates, you can see that the technique has been unsuccessful.

The Footbonaut is a challenge. Players compete with each other to get the top score. This also helps to keep them motivated.

It makes the player focus. If players are finding it too easy, the coaches can increase the speed of the machine so that they have to step out of their comfort zone. As the creator of the Footbonaut, Christian Güttler, said: "Repetition and intensity are crucial if you want to conquer a skill."

Wouldn't it be useful if there was a name for this type of smart training that Pulisic and the other Borussia Dortmund players swear by, training that provides a challenge and makes you step out of your comfort zone?

Well, someone got there first. Super-smart training is called **purposeful practice.**

# MAKE IT PURPOSEFUL

If you only practise what you're comfortable with, then you won't ever get better. Purposeful practice makes you slow down, focus on points you have yet to master, then helps you really hone your technique. You're going to make mistakes. But, in purposeful practice, mistakes are good. They give you a chance to step back and work out what's going wrong, just like in the feedback loop we learned about earlier.

But we know what you're probably thinking right now: "Purposeful practice sounds great, but what if I don't have £2.5 million lying around to buy myself a special robot football machine for the back garden? What else can I do?"

Well, here's the fantastic news: you can do purposeful practice anywhere, any time, and all you need is a ball. Yes, Pulisic used to practise his first touch in the Footbonaut, but he doesn't use a fancy football machine to work on his weaker foot. "Every day in training, even if it's just a simple passing drill, I try to do as many with my left as I do with my right." See? The best players always find new (and purposeful) ways to make themselves even better.

# BECOME A HERO ↘

It's time to practise with purpose. We're going to use the example of control, but you can do it with anything. Keepy-uppies are an excellent way to improve control. Just fifteen minutes of practice a day will give you thousands of touches of the ball each week.

⚽ Start by kicking the ball in the air once, letting it bounce, then kicking it again. See how many times you can do this before losing control. To help, try and send the ball directly upwards and keep it below head height.

⚽ Once you feel comfortable doing keepy-uppies with a bounce, try doing two kicks before letting the ball bounce. This is called progression, which basically means making the skill harder because you're getting better. It's an important part of learning any new skill. Use both feet.

⚽ Eventually, you'll be able to do loads of keepy-uppies with two touches. The next step is to do them with no bounces! Write down your scores so you keep track of your progress and set yourself targets.

⚽ Challenge your team-mates to see who can do the most. To make it more fun, you can even try and do some mad skills with your keepy-uppies, like an around the world.

But what if you're still in your comfort zone? What if you don't feel you're being challenged? Well, we've got the perfect solution. Instead of a football, use a tennis ball. The smaller area means your control has to be super good. And if that's not challenging enough, you can use something even smaller, such as a golf ball!

**TOP TIP:** Always finish your training session on a success. It could be a goal or a new high score for keepy-uppies, for example. This makes you feel happier about the session and means you'll look forward to the next one.

Now you know how purposeful practice works, it's time to test your new-found knowledge.

# QUIZ TIME

## Which player is training smarter?

**Player A:** Takes ten free kicks for ten minutes each day. Trains with a whole bag full of footballs. Analyses each free kick to see how well their technique is working and if there is anything they could improve. Keeps a record of any mistakes and any amazing free kicks. Uses mannequins for a defensive wall and finds a goalkeeper who is four years older and one of the best players in the local area. Remains fully focused on the task. Includes challenges such as: hit the top right corner in four of the next five free kicks.

**Player B:** Takes twenty free kicks in an hour a week. Only brings one football and has to keep on fetching it. No goalkeeper or defensive wall. Spends time between free kicks watching funny videos on YouTube. Quickly forgets mistakes and only focuses on success (so they can tell all their mates).

The answer is Player A, of course! They're in full purposeful-practice mode. They are even starting to feel comfortable feeling uncomfortable!

After all of that purposeful practice, you'll have had hundreds of thousands of touches. You'll feel confident controlling passes in varied and random conditions, just like Pulisic, which will help you to master skills even quicker! Even better, you'll feel comfortable being uncomfortable because there's nothing you love more than a challenge. By now, you'll be building up quite the skill level. But did you know that you've been getting better at football without doing any actual football training? If you transfer over to the next page, we'll show you how.

# HARNESS YOUR HOBBIES

So, who's up for stamp collecting? Chess, anyone? Or how about climbing a few trees in your local park?

> **Wait – I thought this was a book about FOOTBALL?**

It is, we promise! But lots of experts believe that it is best to have a range of different hobbies. That's because you can learn important lessons from each one. Even stamp collecting! Collecting stamps takes discipline, observation and organization. These skills are all really important in football. If you learn them in stamp collecting and then use them to improve your football performance, they become **transferable skills**.

Are you still with us? If not, think about transferable skills in the same way as a football transfer. **Nikita Parris** developed her clinical goal-scoring at Manchester City before she was transferred to Lyon. When she played her first game for Lyon, she took the skills that she learned at Manchester City with her.

There are lots of other fun hobbies you could try that will challenge you in different ways:

CHESS

PAINTING

READING

STAMP COLLECTING

COOKING

CYCLING

DANCING

OK, back to transferable skills, and back to school. Sorry, just for a few minutes!

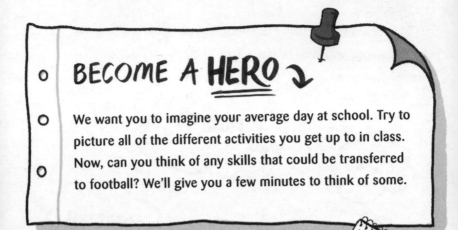

# BECOME A HERO ↴

We want you to imagine your average day at school. Try to picture all of the different activities you get up to in class. Now, can you think of any skills that could be transferred to football? We'll give you a few minutes to think of some.

Done?

OK, here are a few that we came up with:

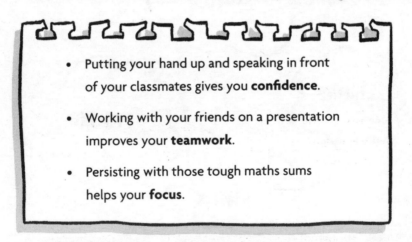

- Putting your hand up and speaking in front of your classmates gives you **confidence**.

- Working with your friends on a presentation improves your **teamwork**.

- Persisting with those tough maths sums helps your **focus**.

Right, let's transfer those skills onto the football pitch:

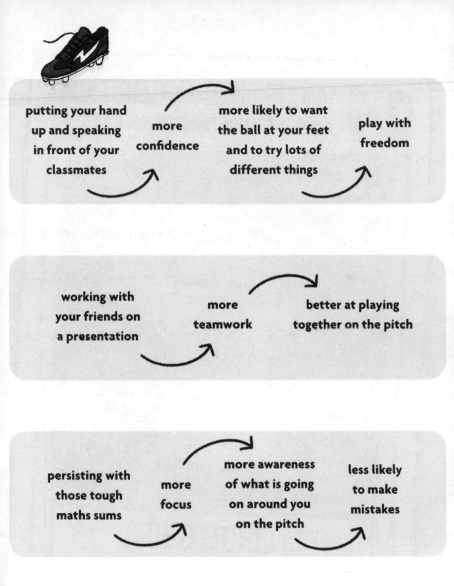

putting your hand up and speaking in front of your classmates → more confidence → more likely to want the ball at your feet and to try lots of different things → play with freedom

working with your friends on a presentation → more teamwork → better at playing together on the pitch

persisting with those tough maths sums → more focus → more awareness of what is going on around you on the pitch → less likely to make mistakes

OK, enough of school. Let's get back to the world of sport – that's what we're here for, right?

# 04 TRAIN LIKE SCHMEICHEL
## SHOW OFF YOUR TRANSFERABLE SKILLS

# PETER SCHMEICHEL

**NATIONALITY:** Danish

**POSITION:** Goalkeeper

**HERO MOMENT:** winning the Treble with Manchester United in 1999

# SUPERCHARGE YOUR SKILLS

Did you know that studies have shown that elite athletes only tend to specialize in their chosen sport between the ages of thirteen and fifteen? Many of your heroes played lots of sports when they were growing up before focusing on football. The skills learned in other sports can have unexpected benefits.

Take our hero in this chapter, for example, legendary shot-stopper **Peter Schmeichel**. "Who?" we hear a few of you ask. But not to worry, football history is one of our favourite subjects. You might be more familiar with his son, **Kasper**, who wears the gloves for Leicester City, but back in the 1990s, Peter was actually an even greater goalkeeper (no offence, Kasper!). During his golden days at Manchester United, he won five Premier League titles, three FA Cups and one Champions League trophy, as well as winning Euro 1992 with Denmark.

But in his younger days, before he became a world-famous footballer, Peter also played another sport: handball. In winter in Denmark, the outdoor pitches would be frozen, meaning he could only play football for six months of the year. So he would play handball instead.

Like football, handball is a team game where you have to

protect your own goal and try to score in your opponent's goal. So far, so familiar, but for the outfield players, there are some pretty major differences. For example, when a player runs with the ball, they have to bounce it, and no one is allowed in the goal area other than the goalkeeper. The most major difference of all? You can only score with your hands!

For a goalkeeper like Schmeichel, however, the two sports are not so different. In fact, through playing handball, he was able to learn lots of transferable skills that he then used to great effect on the football pitch. In handball, the goals are much smaller, and players tend to score from

closer range, which means that goalkeepers have to be very smart and very brave to stop the ball.

Well, Schmeichel was both of those things and more. He became brilliant at tricking the attacker into making the first move. He quickly learned that if he dived too early, it made it much easier for his opponent to score. But if instead he waited, ready to pounce, he put more pressure on the attacker and he had a better chance of predicting where the ball was going to end up.

Schmeichel was also totally fearless. Again and again, he saved the day for Manchester United by flying off his line to perform his famous star jump, where he spread his arms and legs as wide as possible.

By making himself look really big and the goal look really small, he made it so much harder for strikers to score against him. Just ask Alan Shearer and Ian Wright, who both picked Schmeichel as the greatest Premier League goalkeeper of all time on the Match of the Day Top 10 podcast in 2020.

And where did the "Great Dane" get his game-changing move from? "The star jump technique – that is a big part of being a handball goalkeeper and I brought that move into football," he said, adding "... this technique helps you to cover as much of the goal as possible."

So yes, if it hadn't been for handball, Schmeichel may never have become such a legend. And he's far from the only football star who has transferred skills from one sport to another. **Wayne Rooney** was a good boxer, **Gareth Bale** an excellent sprinter, **Alex Morgan** a talented basketball player.

Here are just a few of the transferable skills that you can take from other sports:

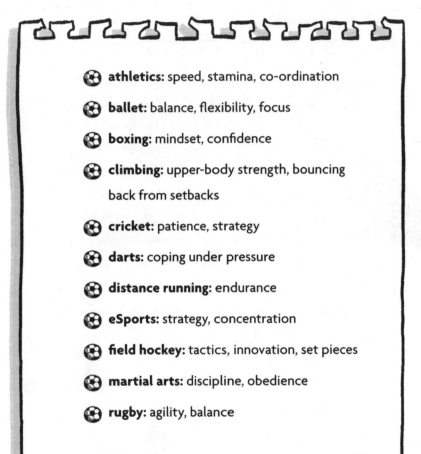

- 🌑 **athletics:** speed, stamina, co-ordination
- 🌑 **ballet:** balance, flexibility, focus
- 🌑 **boxing:** mindset, confidence
- 🌑 **climbing:** upper-body strength, bouncing back from setbacks
- 🌑 **cricket:** patience, strategy
- 🌑 **darts:** coping under pressure
- 🌑 **distance running:** endurance
- 🌑 **eSports:** strategy, concentration
- 🌑 **field hockey:** tactics, innovation, set pieces
- 🌑 **martial arts:** discipline, obedience
- 🌑 **rugby:** agility, balance

Some of these skills are to do with how you think, others are about tactics, the rest are physical improvements you can develop like speed or strength.

And it isn't just the top players that are at it. Football managers take ideas from other sports and transfer them to football.

- Manchester City manager Pep Guardiola's trusted assistant **Manuel Estiarte** is a Spanish water-polo legend.
- Former Huddersfield manager **Danny Cowley** taught PE before becoming a professional football manager.
- Southampton hired former England rugby manager **Clive Woodward** as their performance director.
- "**Total football**" – a way of playing made famous by the Dutch football team in the 1970s – drew on the basics of field hockey. The Dutch coaches saw how hockey players used passing triangles to attack, changed positions all the time to create confusion in the other team and scored lots of goals from set pieces. They then took those tactics and used them in football.

As the story of Peter Schmeichel shows, playing sports other than football can help you to learn new ideas and develop transferable skills. They can also give you a mental rest from playing football and help you to become even more motivated when you return to playing football. So, what will you choose to do?

# BECOME A HERO ↵

Make a list of a few new hobbies you'd like to try and come up with some reasons why they might help you develop transferable skills for football – then give them a go!

Remember, some transferable skills will be more useful in football than others. The discipline that comes from stamp collecting is important, but not as useful as learning to sprint really fast in athletics. Trying lots of different hobbies helps you to find out the best skills that you can then transfer to football – and the ones that you enjoy most. Think of it as scouting. Football clubs scout all over the world for the best players they can transfer to their team. You can scout lots of different hobbies and transfer the best skills into your game.

# 05 TRAIN LIKE PELÉ
## FIND YOUR FLAIR WITH FUTSAL

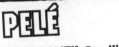

# PELÉ

**NATIONALITY:** Brazilian

**POSITION:** Forward

**HERO MOMENT:** scoring two goals in the 1958 World Cup Final for Brazil, aged only seventeen!

When you think of Brazilian footballers, you immediately think of skills. There's **Neymar** and his famous rainbow flicks, **Ronaldinho**'s flip flaps, **Cristiano Ronaldo**'s stepovers. Brazilians believe there's a simple reason for their skills. It's not their energy-fuelled diet of rice and beans, or their famous samba dancing style, which is all about hip movement. It's a game called futsal.

## WHAT IS FUTSAL?

Essentially, it's a five-a-side version of football played indoors that originated in Brazil in the 1930s (at first it was known as futebol de salão, or hall/lounge football). The goals are narrow and the pitch is smaller. The ball is also smaller and has a weight in it so that it doesn't bounce. This creates a game where the ball moves seven times faster than in football. If the ball goes out of play, it must be kicked back in rather than thrown. Players have just four seconds to get the ball back in play.

Futsal is the ultimate sport for learning transferable skills for football. You don't have to take our word for it; just ask **Edson Arantes do Nascimento**. Who? Sorry, you might know him better as **Pelé**, arguably the greatest footballer of all time.

Aged fourteen, Pelé was a talented young forward playing for his local football club, Bauru, when futsal started taking off. Woah, what was this new indoor game that everyone was talking about? Pelé was desperate to find out, so he signed up for his city's first-ever competition. At first, the organizers told him that he was too young to play with the adults but eventually, they let him join in. And guess what! His team won and he finished as the tournament's top scorer!

Because the play is so quick and the area is smaller, players have less time on the ball. This means that they have to think quickly before they are surrounded by defenders. From the start, Pelé loved everything about futsal, but especially the speed. "Futsal was important in helping to develop my ball control, quick-thinking, passing ... also for dribbling, balance, concentration... Futsal was very, very important..." he said.

When Pelé went back to the football pitch, there was no stopping him. At the age of fifteen, he signed for Santos

and at the age of seventeen, he scored two goals in the final to win the 1958 World Cup for Brazil. A superstar was born. He went on to win two more World Cups and score a phenomenal 1,279 goals!

Of course, Pelé was already a super-talented footballer, but futsal really helped him to develop his skills. He says so himself: "Futsal requires you to think and play fast. It makes everything easier when you later switch to football."

And it's not just Brazilian legends who love it. **Ronaldo** played futsal growing up in Portugal, admitting that "If it wasn't for futsal, I wouldn't be the player I am today." **Messi** agreed: "[Futsal] was tremendous fun, and it really helped me become who I am today."

# WHAT FUTSAL TEACHES US ABOUT FOOTBALL

As well as thinking fast, futsal players also have to be comfortable with the ball at their feet. In a game of futsal, players get twelve times as many touches of the ball as they do in a game of football. Because each team only has four outfield players on the pitch at any one time, everyone plays in all positions. In fact, everyone should be able to attack and defend, even the goalkeeper, or the "fifth man" as they call it in Brazil.

That's the position that Brazilian goalkeeper **Ederson** played during his early days as a futsal star. Often, the fifth man stays deep to defend, but when the coach saw that Ederson had a really powerful shot and an accurate pass, he encouraged him to push forward whenever possible, and he became one of his team's top attackers too.

So far, Ederson has never transferred those shooting skills from the futsal court to the football pitch, but he uses his impressive playmaking skills all the time. He's so comfortable with the ball at his feet that he's like an extra outfield player for his team. He can rush out of his penalty area to clear away danger like a defender, plus he can ping perfect passes – long or short – like a midfielder.

"I think futsal helped me a lot when I was eleven or twelve years old," Ederson said. "It helped me to think quicker and look for the passing lines."

When Seth arrived in Brazil to play professional football, he couldn't believe how skilful the other players on his team were. They were nutmegging him all of the time and making him look silly — even the goalkeepers! Thanks to futsal, Seth's team-mates were comfortable on the ball, happy to defend and attack and always willing to try a skill in training or a match.

When Seth got back to England, his team-mates had taught him so many skills that he was called up to play in the England Under-21s futsal team (that's right, England has a futsal team!). And not only that, his football game had improved too. "You can play 360 degrees now," Seth's manager said. "You're happy to receive possession anywhere and can now attack almost as well as you defend. Futsal is really helping you."

Let us tell you a story about a player Seth had some epic encounters with on the futsal court. Back then, not many people knew him. But they certainly do now!

# Football Fairy Tale:
## The Player Who Owes It All to Futsal

Once upon a time, a boy called Max dreamed of becoming a football player. But after being released by Fulham's academy, then Gillingham's academy, it seemed like his dream was a long way away. But not all was lost, because he had discovered futsal. "I kind of took up futsal just to play to get my fitness up and to become a better player for football," Max said. While the door kept on being closed on him in his football career, his futsal career was on the up.

Soon, Max was training with the England senior team and had transferred to the most successful futsal team in the country: London Helvecia. While training twice a week and playing at the weekends for Helvecia and England, he continued to play football. He signed for Maidenhead United in England's sixth division, who then sent him on loan to eighth division Marlow. As Max picked up more and more caps for England's futsal team, he began to think about becoming a professional futsal player instead.

Then his lucky moment arrived. When he was playing futsal for England, Max was spotted by Wolverhampton Wanderers' head of academy scouting, who took an instant interest in the young player's technical ability and quick-thinking (skills he had honed on the futsal court). Max worked his way into the first team and was soon playing in the Premier League. And he's got futsal to thank!

THE END.

# BECOME A HERO ⤸

The beauty of futsal is that it can be played anywhere.
Maybe your school runs a regular session, or there's a
local club. You could even go to your local multi-sport
court in the park. So give it a go! And when you do,
make sure you use our top tips below so that you can
enjoy the full benefits of the ultimate transferable skill.

## TOP TIPS FOR FUTSAL:

⚽ **Use lots of touches!** Simply passing and controlling
a futsal ball will improve your ball control. Because
the ball is weighted, it is harder to control. The same
goes for shooting. If you practise shooting with a
futsal ball and then switch to a football, you'll find
that your shots are more powerful.

⚽ **Move, move, move.** When you play a futsal game,
you'll find that you can never stand still. If you pass
the ball, you're forced to move into space. Because
there are fewer players, every movement becomes

even more important. When you return to playing football, you'll find that you have loads of space to receive passes.

⚽ **Attack, defend, attack, defend.** Make sure you play all over the pitch rather than sticking to just one position. If you're a defender in football, playing as an attacker in futsal will help you to understand how attackers think.

⚽ **Play with freedom.** Don't worry about the result of the game. Use futsal as a chance to try new skills. If they work, you can transfer them to football where you'll have more time and space!

And futsal isn't the only variation of eleven-a-side football that helps to develop your skills. While **Pelé**, **Neymar** and **Ronaldo** all learned on the futsal court, they also picked up loads of skills by playing street football, just like the following superstar.

# STORY OF A SUPERSTAR

# JADON SANCHO

## THE ULTIMATE TRAINING PRO

O K, are you ready to get out there and train smart like your heroes? We hope so! But just before you lace up your boots or start building your own robot football machine, we're going to tell you a story.

It's about an amazing young winger who you might have heard of – **Jadon Sancho**. Yes, that's right, the superstar who said no to Manchester City and moved to Germany instead, to become Borussia Dortmund's danger man. For this tale, we're going right back to the beginning, to show you Jadon's journey to the top and all the hard work and training along the way.

Jadon grew up in Kennington, South London, where a football was never far from his little feet. From pretty much the moment he could walk, he was always practising. Back then, Jadon's favourite player in the world was Ronaldinho. He would watch videos of the Brazilian's best tricks, from flip flaps to backheel nutmegs. Jadon was determined to become that brilliant, no matter how much training it took.

So, Jadon set to work. Once he had finally mastered the basics on his own (constant conditions, remember?), then he would test his new tricks out in one-on-ones against his mates. And not just a few times; over and over again. After that, it was on to the main event – the epic football matches that took place on the caged pitch on the estate where he lived.

At first, the bigger boys went easy on Jadon because he was so young and small, but he wasn't afraid to make them look like fools. After a few cheeky nutmegs, they soon started taking him seriously. "Woah, how did he do that?" they marvelled. "That kid's got skills!"

When he was seven years old, Jadon's talent was spotted by Watford and he started training at their youth academy three times a week. But that didn't stop him playing street football too. No way! Street football was so much fun, and it was also helping him to become a better player.

Their epic games had no rules and no referees – just rush keepers and way too many players crammed onto a tiny concrete pitch. It was end-to-end chaos and Jadon loved it! He never had much time or space to try out his tricks, but that's what made it so challenging. He was always out of his comfort zone, but the more he played and the more he dared to take on the defenders (some of them much bigger!), the faster his mind and feet moved.

In street football, he was free to express himself, to use trial and error and show off his latest skills without worrying about what his Watford coach would say. If the new skill went well and he scored, great! He would use it again. And if it didn't go so well and he lost the ball, never mind! Jadon would just keep practising and make changes to improve his technique until he discovered what worked best for him.

It didn't matter if he got something wrong. Street football was all about being creative and trying new things.

Jadon learned a lot from his street football battles – how to get back up when the bigger boys fouled him, how to keep hold of the ball in tight spaces and how to think fast. But most of all, street football gave Jadon the confidence to take his tricks and transfer them into proper football matches. With those skills from street football, combined with the tactical lessons he learned at Watford, Jadon now looked unstoppable.

At the age of fifteen, he signed for Manchester City and started working his way towards the first team. Jadon learned lots from training with some of the top youth coaches in the game, and he quickly became one of the academy's brightest stars alongside **Phil Foden**. But as he turned seventeen, a regular first-team spot still seemed a very distant possibility. Jadon wanted to be playing in the Premier League but unfortunately, he had young superstars like **Raheem Sterling**, **Leroy Sané** and **Gabriel Jesus** ahead of him at City. How was he ever going to get game-time?

So, when the club offered Jadon his first professional contract, he made the bold, brave decision to say no and sign for Borussia Dortmund instead. It was time for a new challenge. The German team had a great reputation for developing young stars and giving them the chance to play. Plus, they had just lost two of their top attackers: **Pierre-Emerick Aubameyang** and **Ousmane Dembélé**.

"I'm ready to replace them!" Jadon told himself confidently, taking Dembélé's Number 7 shirt straight away.

During his first year in Germany, Jadon went back and forth between the Dortmund youth team and senior team. Oh, and there were lots of trips to the Footbonaut too, of course! Working hard week after week, Jadon added extra elements to his game, especially touch and decision-making, so that once he got the ball in attacking areas, he already knew what he should do next, whether to pass, cross, or shoot.

As soon as the 2018–19 season started, Jadon showed that he was in the first team to stay. He played with confidence and without fear, as if he were back in Kennington playing street football with his mates. Only now, his skills were even more effective.

Dortmund were drawing 1–1 with Eintracht Frankfurt when the ball came to Jadon out on the right wing. Showtime! First, he dribbled his way into the penalty area at top speed, and then, when two defenders rushed across to tackle him, he turned to his big bag of tricks. He fooled both defenders with one clever Cruyff cut back (basically, a fancy name for a backheel) and then delivered a perfect cross with his weaker left foot. GOAL!

Soon, Jadon was starting every game for Dortmund, even though he was still only eighteen years old. And in October 2018, he got his first call-up to the senior England squad. That's when Jadon knew for sure that it had all been worth it – the long trips to train at Watford, the big move to Manchester City, the decision to sign for Dortmund and, of course, the years of training smart by trying out tricks in the cages of Kennington.

# SO ARE YOU READY TO TRAIN SMART?

Training is simply a way to get better. Everyone – even if your name is Messi – needs to put in the hours if they seriously want to improve.

Training ideas can come from all kinds of places. Watch what others do and see if you can copy anything. Ask your teachers and coaches for ideas. Speak to your friends and team-mates. Search for drills and training plans on YouTube and Instagram. Then go about trying them for yourself. If you enjoy them, then keep on trying them!

When you train, make sure it is purposeful. Activities such as futsal and street football are excellent as they provide a challenge and give you the freedom to have a go at new things. Step out of your comfort zone and try to master skills that you can't yet do well, while still working to improve skills that you have already mastered.

# TOP TEN TIPS FOR TRAINING SMART:

1.  Repetition, repetition, repetition. The more you do something, the better you get.

2.  Have fun! If you enjoy training, then you'll train more often.

3.  Use constant, variable and random training to fully develop a skill.

4.  Become comfortable with feeling uncomfortable. If you never step out of your comfort zone and make mistakes, then you'll never get better.

5.  Seek feedback so you can see how to get better.

6.  Challenge yourself. Once you've beaten the challenge, challenge yourself again.

7.  Train with and against players bigger and better than you. It's one of the best ways to learn quickly.

8.  Look at how other players do skills and see if you can copy them.

9.  Use the skills you learn from other sports and hobbies and even school to help your football ability.

10. Celebrate your achievements. When you nail something you've been practising for ages, reward yourself.

# ULTIMATE CHALLENGES TO TRAIN SMART:

1. Create a square measuring 2 metres x 2 metres and stand inside it. Throw the ball against a wall and control it without your body or the ball leaving the square. Keep track of how many times out of ten you succeed with both your right and left feet. Once this becomes easy, make the square smaller and kick the ball instead of throwing it.

2. Use the feedback loop to find five ways you can improve your five weakest skills.

3. Find the craziest skill you've ever seen your favourite footballer do. Watch it back on YouTube, then try to copy it. Once you've copied it, then try and use it in a game of street football or futsal.

4. Find the best players in your school and play against them on the playground. If you are the best player, then challenge yourself by only using your weak foot in the game.

5. Take a skill you learn in the classroom and transfer it to improve your football ability.

# PLAY WITH YOUR HEAD

Raise your arm as high in the air as you can. Try to touch the ceiling. How far have you got?

Now try and reach even higher. Go on, give it everything!

What happened? We bet that you just stretched even higher – although you already thought your arm was as high as you could reach!

Your mind is an amazing thing. When you've given your all and think that there's nothing left, the power of your mind allows you to go a little bit further. And that's true whether you're reaching as high as you can or you're trying to win a football match.

World Cup winning Italian midfielder **Andrea Pirlo** once said:

**Football is played in the head, while the feet are just the tools.**

And he's right. The very best footballers think smarter than the rest.

Every time you step on the football field, your brain is in for a workout. Before you've even touched the ball, your brain is already busy thinking up lots of different outcomes.

How fast is the ball travelling and which
type of control should I use?

Where is it likely to land?

Where are the opposing defenders and how
likely are they to intercept a pass?

When I get the ball, should I pass, dribble or shoot?

Where are my team-mates and where are
they likely to move to?

How much power should I put on a pass?

And there's more! In a game of football, you don't just
need incredible skills backed up by good decision-making.
You have to think far bigger than just what happens in
ninety minutes on a pitch. To be a truly amazing player,
you need to have the right mindset. That means the way
you approach things in life – not just football. Being
positive has real power.

Do you see a glass as half-full or half-empty? At half-time
do you see the game as half-finished or only half-played?
Those with the right mindset (half-full, half-played) always
see the positive in any situation. The right mindset is what
will give you a better chance of making the right decision
in the madness of a match.

To achieve the same mindset as a top footballer, you need to have:

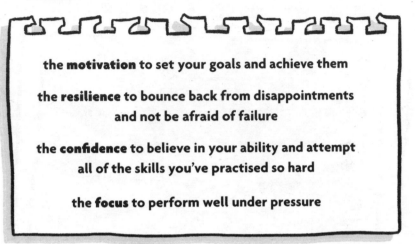

the **motivation** to set your goals and achieve them

the **resilience** to bounce back from disappointments and not be afraid of failure

the **confidence** to believe in your ability and attempt all of the skills you've practised so hard

the **focus** to perform well under pressure

Does that sound like a long and difficult list? Well, don't worry, we're now going to show you *how* to think smart, just like your heroes.

# 01 THINK LIKE MIEDEMA

## SET YOUR GOALS, THEN SCORE THEM

# VIVIANNE MIEDEMA

**NATIONALITY:** Dutch

**POSITION:** Forward

**HERO MOMENT:** scoring two goals for the Netherlands in the UEFA Women's Euro 2017 final

The very best footballers in the world think about amazing goals, then go and score them. But not only in the way you are imagining.

To these footballers, goals aren't just numbers you score. When you think smart, goals are things that you want to achieve. They're your aims, dreams and ambitions. And having aims, dreams and ambitions keeps you focused on what you want and gives you the motivation to train smart. Which then makes you more likely to achieve them!

Take **Vivianne Miedema**, the star striker for Arsenal and the Netherlands national team. She was only fifteen when she achieved her first goal of becoming a professional footballer for her local team, Heerenveen. But she didn't stop there; no, she kept setting herself new, bigger targets to aim for:

1. **Become the top scorer in the league** – Miedema scored thirty-nine goals during the 2013–14 BeNe League season (a whopping fifteen more than the next-highest scorer, and she was still only seventeen!).

2. **Play for my country** – She made her Netherlands debut in September 2013.

3. **Move to a bigger club** – She joined German giants Bayern Munich in June 2014.

4. **Win a league title** – She won the Bundesliga title twice at Bayern, before moving to Arsenal and winning the Women's Super League too. ✓

5. **Win an international trophy** – She helped the Netherlands to win the UEFA Women's Euro 2017, scoring the winning goal in the semi-finals against England and two more in the final against Denmark. ✓

6. **Score fifty goals for the Netherlands** – Amazingly, she achieved this aim in 2018! ✓

7. **Become the Netherlands' record goal-scorer** – She overtook the previous record of fifty-nine goals in 2019 and is already well on her way towards her next 100-goal target. ✓

8. **Win the Women's World Cup and the Champions League** – She's still working towards these targets, which are every footballer's greatest goals. ✗

So, as you can see, Miedema is a scoring machine who keeps herself motivated by always having a new goal to aim towards. And her goals come in all shapes, sizes and time frames. Yes, she wants to finish next season with the league title and the top scorer trophy, but each and every week, she also sets herself a small goal that she knows she can achieve. She says, "I'm going on the pitch to try and win the game."

# HOW TO SET YOUR GOALS ...

A good goal is one that you're in full control of. It should be hard, but not so hard that you'll never be able to achieve it. This helps you to get out of your comfort zone, which we know is an important part of helping you get better at football.

But having some easy goals is also a good idea. That's because when you achieve a goal, you feel a warm sense of achievement. *Tick!* Feels pretty great, doesn't it? You'll want to keep working at scoring the small goals and then eventually you'll score a bigger one that is much more challenging. *TICK!*

Maybe you just want to work on a new skill for ten minutes every day in a week. This is called a **short-term goal**, because it's an ambition you want to achieve in a short period of time.

A **medium-term goal** is a target that will take a bit longer to achieve – anything from a week to several months – something like Miedema aiming to win the Women's Super League Player of the Month award, for example.

Finally, a **long-term goal** is anything that will take longer than three months to do, like Miedema winning the Ballon d'Or.

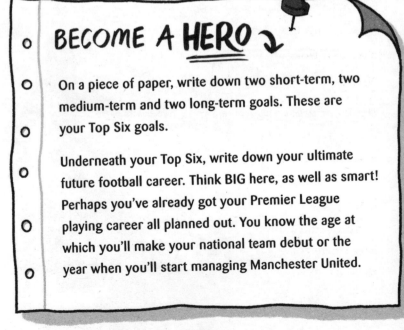

## BECOME A **HERO** ↴

On a piece of paper, write down two short-term, two medium-term and two long-term goals. These are your Top Six goals.

Underneath your Top Six, write down your ultimate future football career. Think BIG here, as well as smart! Perhaps you've already got your Premier League playing career all planned out. You know the age at which you'll make your national team debut or the year when you'll start managing Manchester United.

## ... AND HOW TO SCORE THEM

Hopefully, you've gone massive like Miedema and aimed for goals that you really, really want to achieve. Great! Having big ambitions helps drive you to success. But does your goal list look a bit scary now that it's written down on paper? Does it feel like it'll take ages to complete? Maybe it seems just too far out of reach?

Don't worry, because now that you've worked out **what** your goals are, it's time to think about **when** you want to achieve them and **how** you're going to do it.

As the famous sports psychiatrist, Dr Steve Peters, says, "a goal without a plan is just a dream". It's only by breaking your dream into smaller, much more achievable goals, that it becomes more real. If you know how you'll achieve your goal, you'll actually start to make progress.

Let's go back to Miedema for a minute. Once she had set herself that tricky long-term target of scoring fifty goals for the Netherlands, she then had to work out how she was going to get there. How was she going to become one of the best goal-scorers in the game? By practising hard at her:

### Sharp shooting

When she was younger, Miedema kept injuring her right ankle and so she learned to shoot really well with her weaker left foot too. Now, she's brilliant at scoring with both feet and that makes her doubly dangerous because defenders don't know which way she'll go!

### Close control

Growing up, Miedema's ultimate football hero was former Arsenal and Manchester United striker, **Robin van Persie**. The Dutchman was famous for his phenomenal first touch and now so is Miedema, thanks to all her training at keeping the ball in small, tight spaces.

Without training, it'll be very hard for you to achieve your goals. But knowing what your goals are will help you to plan what type of training to do. For example, if you want to be signed by an elite team but need to become more confident with the ball at your feet, you know that you need to work on your control and dribbling.

## BECOME A HERO ↴

Take your list of Top Six goals and make them more achievable by adding the when and the how. Just like Miedema, start with a long-term goal and break it down into medium- and short-term goals to work out how you'll achieve it. Your list should look something like this:

- Short-term goal: work on my shooting for twenty minutes every day this week by practising against the best goalkeeper I know and using the feedback loop to perfect my technique.

- Medium-term goal: score five goals in the next ten games by working at all of the different shooting techniques I learn.

- Long-term goal: become my school football team's number one striker by the start of next season.

Now you've taken control of your dreams. By writing them down, you've already made them more real. You can even stick the list up on your wall so you keep seeing it. That way, it will make you more **focused** and more **motivated** to work hard in training.

As you train to achieve your goal, record your progress. If your goal is to do 100 keepy-uppies without dropping the ball, write down how many you manage in each training session. You might not get a higher score every single day you train, but by the end of the week you should be able to do more than you could at the start of the week.

The task doesn't get easier. You get better.

It takes time, effort and persistence to achieve a goal. When you do achieve a goal, make sure you enjoy that feeling of success, even if, like Miedema, you're not a fan of big goal celebrations! This could be by telling friends and family or even rewarding yourself by watching a film you've wanted to see for ages or playing your favourite video game. But goals don't stop at a celebration. Once you've achieved one goal, it's time to set a new goal. Think smart like Miedema – your next goal should be even more challenging than the last. And always remember your ultimate goal!

Even if you don't quite achieve all of your goals, it's still great to have something detailed to work towards and a plan of how to get there. Simply by sticking to that plan, you'll become a better player. And as we're about to find out, sometimes failing to achieve your goal can actually work out for the best.

# 02 THINK LIKE SALAH

## BOUNCE BACK FROM DISAPPOINTMENTS

# MO SALAH

**NATIONALITY:** Egyptian

**POSITION:** Forward

**HERO MOMENT:** scoring Liverpool's first goal in the Champions League final in 2019

# FAILURE!

Ooh, that looks scary, doesn't it?

OK, how about this: **FAILURE?**

Not so bad, right? To think smart, we need to change how
we see failure. Let us tell you about **Mohamed** (or "**Mo**"
as fans call him) **Salah**. You've heard of him, right? He's the
Egyptian King who can't stop scoring. While he's been at
Liverpool, he's won the Premier League, the Champions
League, the Golden Boot two years in a row and he's been
named African Footballer of the Year twice.

But did you know that Salah actually played in the Premier
League before he played for Liverpool? Back in 2014, he
signed for Chelsea, but in his first two seasons at the club,
he only played nineteen games and scored just two goals!

**José Mourinho**, the Chelsea manager at the time, didn't
think that Mo was good enough to play for his team. "He
was just a lost kid in London. He was a lost kid in a new
world," he said.

Salah's first spell in England ended in 2015, when he was
sent out on loan to Italian side Fiorentina. Such a step-
down sounds like a failure, right? For some players, it
might have been. For Mo that move ended up being the

beginning of his journey to global superstardom. It was a fresh start for him, away from the pressures of the Premier League, where he could build up his confidence again by playing lots more football.

After months of sitting on the Chelsea bench, suddenly Salah was starting every week for Fiorentina. And starring too. He took Italy by storm, scoring a total of forty-three goals in 109 games for Fiorentina and then his new club Roma (plus twenty-six assists too). He was playing with such quality and confidence that Liverpool offered to pay £42 million euros to bring him back to England.

But was he willing to go? It would have been easy for Salah to say no after his hard time at Chelsea, but instead, he said YES! He understood that failure is an important part of every success. He was ready to step out of his comfort zone to give the Premier League another crack and prove people wrong.

In his first season back, Salah broke all kinds of records. He was named PFA Players' Player of the Year as he scored thirty-two times in thirty-eight Premier League games, while his ten goals in the Champions League catapulted Liverpool into the final. Though the final would end in heartbreak for him as he was stretchered off with a nasty injury, he returned the following season to win the Champions League for Liverpool and show himself to be one of the best players in the world.

The message of that story? Stay strong like Salah! Don't be afraid of failure, because everybody fails. Even the very best players have missed an easy chance or been in a situation where they haven't made the grade. It is how those players reacted to their failures that has gone on to make them the very best.

# BECOME A HERO ↴

So, what about you? Has somebody ever told you that you aren't good enough? Perhaps you fluffed a penalty or lost an important match? On a piece of paper, write down three disappointing or frustrating moments you've experienced when playing football. Now compare them to Mo Salah's disappointing moments. Take inspiration from his story and think how you did – or can – bounce back to become even better!

## LISTENING TO OTHERS

If somebody tells you that you aren't good enough at football, then you haven't failed. That person's opinion is just an opinion, not a fact. Their opinion can be changed – just like Salah changed Mourinho's. "The Salah I knew at Chelsea was a project player. Now he is one of the best in the world," his old manager later admitted.

Use your failures as fuel to prove all those who doubt you wrong, just like Mo did.

Now seems like the perfect time to introduce you to two of Seth's former team-mates, Lucas and Sam, and tell you their story.

# Football Fairy Tale:
## A Tale of Two Players

Once upon a time, Lucas was the best player at Seth's football academy. He even played for the youth side of his national team. Yet at the end of the season, he and another player called Sam were told that they weren't good enough to play for the academy the following season.

Lucas found this failure devastating. He thought that one person's opinion was fact. Maybe he shouldn't bother any more? Perhaps football just wasn't for him.

Sam found this failure motivating. He saw it as a chance to learn. He knew that he would succeed as a footballer. He reflected on why he wasn't considered good enough and planned a training programme to work on his weaknesses. He set goals for what he wanted to achieve. Then he trained hard and trained smart to prove the coach wrong.

One year later, Lucas gave up playing football.

Two years later, Sam signed his first professional contract.

Ten years later, Sam played his first game in the Premier League.

Sam used the disappointment to learn and refocus. Most importantly, he understood the power of "yet". He knew that he wasn't where he wanted to be *yet*, but if he kept thinking smart, he might still get there. The setback made him achieve his dreams. THE END.

# BOUNCING BACK

As the stories of Mo and Sam show, failure shouldn't be a nasty, scary word. Instead, it's an important step on the path to success. If Salah hadn't failed at Chelsea, who knows, maybe he wouldn't have had the mental strength to win the Premier League and Champions League.

And if Sam hadn't failed at his academy, he may never have signed his first professional contract. Yet Sam realized that everyone improves at different speeds. There was still lots of time for him to get taller, faster and stronger. There were thousands of hours for him to study players and strategies and learn from them.

So that's what he did.

When you watch Sam play now, it seems amazing to think that somebody ever said he wasn't good enough. But that actually happened.

Maybe Mo and Sam weren't good enough once, but now they're more than good enough. They've bounced back to become some of the best players on the planet. How? By learning from every experience, good or bad.

When we fail, we have a chance to reflect. Sure, no one likes reliving the moment when something went wrong. But if you don't, you have no chance of learning from it. This is the feedback loop we looked at in Train Smart in action once more. Is it something you can improve through training? Were you not giving enough effort on the day? After reflecting on why the failure happened, you can then refocus on what's important.

## BECOME A HERO ↴

Grab that paper again and take another look at your list of disappointments. For each, ask yourself:

- **Why** did it happen?

- **What** could you have done to prevent the failure?

- **How** will you be more successful next time? Will it be by training smart on your technical weaknesses like Sam did? How about setting goals like Miedema? Or preparing better (more on that in the next chapter)?

Just like Mo and Sam, you too can learn from setbacks. Mo and Sam persisted and planned how to get better. And they did so with the power of one secret ingredient: confidence.

If you think you can or think you can't, you're probably right.

Woah, what? Doesn't that sound like some kind of riddle? Well, fear not, for we are about to explain how it has everything to do with confidence.

Confidence is how likely you feel something is to happen. Let's give it a go. Is there a ball at your feet? Good. Give it a kick. It doesn't matter in which direction. Just kick it. That's easy, right? You've got 100% confidence that you can move your legs in the right direction. You've done it millions of times already in your life. You don't even have to think about doing it. You just know that it's going to happen.

Your mind and your body are closely linked. Because your mind tells you it's easy to move your foot to the ball, your body responds. You believe that you can achieve something and so you achieve it.

When your mind feels good, your body works better. And when you move with confidence, you perform the skill well.

Picture **Kevin De Bruyne**, the Manchester City and Belgium magician, as he prepares to play a defence-splitting pass through to team-mate **Raheem Sterling**.

Most people wouldn't even see the gap, let alone attempt to guide the ball through it. In order to succeed, everything about the pass will have to be perfect: the angle, the power, the accuracy.

So, do you think De Bruyne worries about whether he'll succeed or not? No! He might be quiet and shy off the pitch, but on it, he's full of confidence. He believes in himself and his ability to pull off another amazing assist because he has already done it so many times before.

Without confidence, your talent is far less than it should be.

But with confidence, your talent goes even further than you thought it could. Just look at De Bruyne.

- **Confident people have the courage to step out of their comfort zones and try new experiences.**
  De Bruyne was only fourteen years old when he left his home in Drongen to join the Genk academy, 100 miles away. Can you imagine living that far away from your family? At first, De Bruyne did find it difficult, but he never gave up on his football dream.

- **Confident people also set themselves challenging goals and then train hard to achieve them. They understand the power of "yet".**

When De Bruyne's dream move to Chelsea didn't work out and the club decided to let him leave in 2014, he didn't just give up on playing in the Premier League. No, after two great seasons in Germany, he came back to England with more confidence, to prove people wrong and win lots of trophies at Manchester City.

- **Confident people have no fear of failure. If they do have a setback, they have the self-belief that they will bounce back and improve even more.**

De Bruyne had to miss big chunks of Manchester City's 2018–19 season because of a bad knee injury. But he came back better than ever in 2019–20: more magic, more goals and even more amazing assists!

- **Confident people are shown to keep going even when things seem against them.**

Remember the incredible 2019 Champions League quarter-final second leg, where Tottenham beat Manchester City 4–3? Well, De Bruyne might have finished on the losing team that night, but he still set up three goals for Raheem Sterling and Sergio Agüero!

But here's the best thing about confidence: you don't have to be De Bruyne to have it. You can work on yours too!

# UNLEASH YOUR CONFIDENCE

Confidence is like a superpower; yet every superpower can have its fatal downfall. For confidence, that potential downfall is arrogance. Confidence is knowing that you are good at a skill and understanding that you need to keep training smart to improve that skill. But when that confidence morphs into arrogance, you no longer think that you need to keep on working hard to improve that skill. When that happens, your skills are in danger of going backwards. There's a reason that even the world's best footballers still train every day – they are confident enough to know that they need to keep improving, otherwise all of the other footballers will catch up with them and overtake them.

Confidence comes from experience. The more times you have an experience, the happier you feel about repeating that experience. That means training will improve your ability. Take keepy-uppies. The first time you tried them, you may not have been confident that you could do ten. But after training thirty minutes a day for a month, you'd feel very confident in your ability to do ten.

Yet there's no point in being confident during a training session if your confidence then disappears during a game. This happens to lots of footballers. When they train, they have no fear and they feel confident in their abilities. But in a match, they doubt whether their skills are good enough. They become scared of giving the ball away or missing a tackle. They lose their confidence and take fewer risks. Negative thoughts enter their minds. Simple skills may suddenly seem hard.

Don't fear! Even these players can improve their confidence and we've got three great ways to do it.

# 1. VISUALIZATION

When we form a mental image of ourselves performing a task really well, it makes us more confident that we will be able to do that task in the future. If we've already succeeded, we can succeed again. This formation of a mental image is called **visualization**.

Top footballers use visualization before and even during games. Many use it every single day. Some footballers make their mental images super realistic by watching films or YouTube videos of their past performances. You can even record yourself doing a skill well in training and then watch it back to increase your confidence. And visualization isn't just about what's happened in the past. You can also imagine what's going to happen in the game ahead. Picture yourself running across the pitch and receiving a pass. Can you see yourself running past opponents, dribbling past them like they aren't even there? England legend **Wayne Rooney** made his visualization so realistic that he even used to phone up the kit manager the night before a game to ask what colour kit he'd be wearing the next day.

When it finally comes to playing the actual game, your confidence has improved. You've already played really well in your head, which makes you more likely to play really well in reality.

# BECOME A HERO ↴

Think back to the time when you played your best-ever football match. Maybe you scored a wonder goal that went straight in like a De Bruyne free kick, or perhaps you made a goal-saving tackle. Think really hard. Screw up your face if you have to. Good. Now we want you to make it even more real.

- How did the ball feel when it touched your foot?
- What did you see?
- What did you hear?
- What could you taste?
- What could you smell?

That's visualization in action!

Visualization floods your mind with positive thoughts. Having positive thoughts makes your body feel better. And when your body feels better, it relaxes. This makes it easier to carry out your skills to the best of your ability. So, give it a go, next time you're out on the football field.

## 2. SELF-TALK

The mind is a powerful tool in making us more confident, and so is the mouth. It feels great when somebody tells us how good we are, or how they are sure that we can succeed. But what about if that somebody is YOU?

"What? You want me to talk to myself?!" It sounds strange, but lots of your football heroes do it, so why shouldn't you too? It's called **self-talk**. For example:

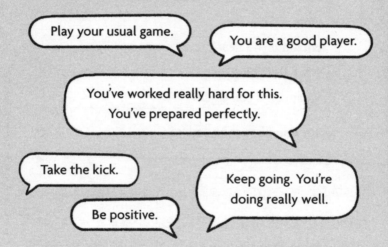

Play your usual game.

You are a good player.

You've worked really hard for this. You've prepared perfectly.

Take the kick.

Keep going. You're doing really well.

Be positive.

Some of these examples are instructions. They remind you of what is needed in the game ahead. Others are encouraging, reminding you of your talent. Both of these types of self-talk improve your confidence as they fill your mind with positive thoughts.

# BECOME A **HERO** ↴

Try some self-talk before and during your next match or training session. Mix things up: instructions and inspirational words, speaking both out loud and in your head. That way, you'll see what works best for you.

## 3. BODY LANGUAGE

And it isn't just your words that can increase your confidence. So does your **body language** – how your body looks on the pitch.

Our bodies communicate our feelings.

Some people go red when they speak in class. This means that they're embarrassed. What about people who look directly into the eyes of those they're speaking to? This means that they're confident and trusting.

# QUIZ TIME

**Which of these two players is the most confident?**

**Player A:** Shuffles onto the pitch, head down and shoulders hunched. They glance over at the opposition and then put their head down once more. Their face is a grimace.

**Player B:** Runs onto the pitch as if they own it. Their chest is stuck out and their head is held high. Their body is taking up as much space as possible. There is a huge smile on their face.

The answer is obvious, right? It's Player B!

Next time you watch Manchester City play, keep a close eye on De Bruyne's body language. Does he look scared or nervous? No! His chest is puffed out and his head is held high. He's Mr Confident!

# BECOME A HERO ↴

When you're out on the football pitch, try standing a bit taller, relaxing your shoulders and sticking your chest out with a big smile. Even if you don't feel particularly confident, looking confident is infectious. Looking and acting confident will make you feel more confident, and it will also make your team-mates feel much more confident too. Double win!

Negative thoughts will always enter a player's head. You'll wonder if you can play well and perform under pressure. But the best footballers like De Bruyne use techniques like visualization, self-talk and positive body language to help remove those negative thoughts. They fill their minds with positive thoughts instead.

When you think positive, you become more confident. When you become more confident, you are more likely to perform well and reach your goals. This is because confidence allows us to express ourselves – even in front of thousands of fans.

So, what do you think to that riddle now? **Can** you, or **can't** you? That's right: of course you **can**!

# 04 THINK LIKE MARADONA
## PERFORM UNDER PRESSURE

## DIEGO MARADONA

**NATIONALITY:** Argentinian

**POSITION:** Attacking Midfielder

**HERO MOMENT:** leading Argentina to World Cup glory in 1986 with his sublime skills

Let's start by imagining a scene.

*It's the final minute of the biggest game of the season. Your striker has just been fouled in the penalty area and the referee has pointed to the penalty spot.*

*You're the penalty taker.*

*If you score the penalty, your team will win the league. If you miss, your team will only finish second.*

*How will you react?*

This is called a pressure situation. The footballer knows it's essential they perform well but the pressure can lead to nerves and worries. These make it harder to do what they need to do and may lead the footballer to "choke", which is when their performance totally collapses (also known as "having a stinker, shocker or a nightmare").

When Brazil played Germany in the 2014 World Cup semi-final, they choked. The whole country expected Brazil to win. The players sung the national anthem at the start of the match along with their supporters. They high-fived each other and got into their positions ahead of kick-off.

And then they lost 7–1.

The team didn't function as usual. The players felt under pressure to meet the fans' expectations. They moved in the wrong positions. Even the simplest of skills went wrong. It was as if the players shrunk.

Pressure is part of every football match. Parents and supporters shout on the sidelines. Opponents get in your face. Your coach asks you to carry out instructions. Your team-mates demand the ball. Everyone wants to win!

When you are faced with pressure, there are two ways to respond. You can be like Brazil in 2014 and see the pressure situation as a threat to your confidence and a chance to fail. Or you can be like **Diego Maradona**, nicknamed Argentina's "Golden Boy", and see pressure as a challenge and a chance to stand out.

During the 1980s, Maradona was not only his country's best player, but also the best player on the planet. With the ball at his feet, he could dribble past any defender, or even sometimes, a whole team of defenders!

Being that good at football, however, meant that the fans expected a lot from him. Argentinians love football almost as much as Brazilians (if you don't believe us, just ask Messi!). The whole country expected him to win the 1986 World Cup for them – on his own if he had to.

"It's very difficult to be Maradona," his Argentina team-mate, Jorge Valdano, once said. "The pressure he lives under, no one in the history of football has had to go through that."

But despite all that pressure, "El Diego" did it! In 1986, Maradona led his otherwise pretty average national team all the way past:

- England in the quarters (let's not talk about his first goal – *cough* handball *cough* – but the second was an absolute worldie!)
- Belgium in the semis (two more magnificent goals)
- West Germany in the final (zero goals but an amazing assist to set up the winner)

El Diego had done it – Argentina were the Champions of the World! And as if that wasn't enough, Maradona then took the national team all the way to the final again in 1990 (even with a bad toe injury), but this time they lost 1–0 to West Germany.

So, Maradona really took his chance to stand out on the international stage, but what about his club career? Well, there was plenty of pressure there too. When he arrived at Napoli in 1984, 75,000 excited fans filled the stadium to

welcome him. The passionate local people were desperate for their club to win their first-ever Italian league title, and now they had a superstar who was going to lead them all the way to the top of Serie A. They expected Maradona to work his magic again, just like he had for Argentina.

Pressure, what pressure? El Diego did it – twice! And on top of two league titles, Maradona's Napoli also won the Coppa Italia and the UEFA Cup too. No wonder the locals love him so much!

But how did Maradona do it? Simple: by thinking positively about pressure.

He treated each big game as a good thing, a challenge for him to complete. After all, pressure is a privilege. If we feel pressure, that means that what we're doing matters. It'd be boring going through life without doing anything important.

When we feel pressure, our hearts race and our palms get clammy. We may even feel sick with nerves. These feelings are all good. Our body knows that what we're about to do is important and so it starts to prepare. Footballers who see pressure as a challenge turn their anxiety into excitement. They look forward to standing out against good players. They can't wait to overcome the challenge, just like they do in their training sessions.

## HOW TO HANDLE PRESSURE

Our attitudes and emotions decide our actions. You can control the effort you put into training ahead of a game. You can control the effort you put into the game. You can make sure you play with a smile on your face. You can even control your confidence.

Focus on what you can do rather than what you can't.

Don't say "don't". OK, we just broke that rule. But let us tell you why.

Don't think about an alien in a Chelsea kit. Whatever you do, don't think about the alien! No, seriously, don't!

Are you thinking about the alien?

We bet you probably are, even when we told you not to. So what do you think happens when you tell yourself not to give the ball away, or not to miss the penalty?

When you think about not messing up, it actually makes you more likely to mess up.

# BECOME A HERO

The next time you're feeling nervous about a big game, give these tips a go:

**1. Act confident (even if you don't feel it)**

You already learned all about this in the previous section. To play your best game in pressure situations, you have to approach every game with a confident attitude.

**2. Focus on yourself and no one else**

You cannot control what your team-mates or the opponents do. You cannot control the pitch or the weather. Time spent thinking about the things you cannot control takes your mind away from the things that you can control.

**3. Remember why you play football in the first place**

As Maradona once said, "That's where the fun is: on the pitch with the ball. That's what I've always done, whether at Wembley or the Maracanã, with a hundred thousand people watching." El Diego's right: football is something to enjoy, not something to be scared of. So make sure you play with a big smile on your face! If you look happy, you're more likely to feel happy, which will then help your body to relax.

And if it goes wrong? Remember, failure isn't a bad thing, anyway. Even the very best sometimes fail in pressure situations. Maradona missed a penalty against Yugoslavia in a quarter-final shoot-out at the 1990 World Cup, while his fellow Argentinian magician, Messi, has missed twenty-six in his career. In 2012 he lost possession of the ball more than any other player in the whole of La Liga. That's not what he'll be remembered for.

Confident footballers see failure as bad but not terrible. They've already failed millions of times in their lives and lived to tell the tale. They want to succeed but don't see it as essential. They trust that if they work hard, they'll have a better chance of success. They focus on what they can control, which improves their ability to perform skills under pressure. And they know that everyone is human.

Humans fail. Humans succeed. And football is played against humans, not against teams of aliens sent from a galaxy far away. When they know that, pressure doesn't seem too bad. In fact, it seems pretty good.

Confident players take the penalty. They are mentally tough under pressure. They see it as a chance to score and don't assume the keeper will save it. They pick their spot, tune out from the crowd and focus all of their energy on what they can do in that moment. They visualize their success and then use self-talk to increase their confidence. They make a firm connection with the ball.

And if they miss, they'll take the next penalty too.

# STORY OF A SUPERSTAR

# HARRY KANE

## THE ULTIMATE THINKING PRO

This is the story of the ultimate thinking footballer, a hero who has it all: ambition, resilience, confidence, focus and bouncebackability (yes, that is a real word!). This is the story of England captain and Tottenham legend **Harry Kane**!

Harry grew up in Chingford, East London, dreaming of becoming a top professional footballer, just like his heroes, Spurs striker **Teddy Sheringham** and England captain, **David Beckham**. Harry even went to the same school as "Becks" and started out playing for the same local club, Ridgeway Rovers. Surely, it was meant to be!

It certainly looked that way when, aged eight, Harry was scouted and signed by a Premier League club. But no, it wasn't his beloved Tottenham; instead, it was their big North London rivals, Arsenal!

Harry loved every minute of his time at the Arsenal academy, but after one season, the club decided that he wasn't tall or fast enough for them. That disappointment must have really hurt, but he didn't give up. He kept working hard on his football skills back at Ridgeway Rovers. He had to be ready for when another, better opportunity came along.

A few years later, during a trial at Watford, Harry got the chance to play against his beloved team Tottenham.

This was the chance that he had been waiting for, and after his Arsenal experience, he wasn't afraid of failure any more. With the pressure on, he proved that, even at the age of eleven, he already was a big-game player. The Spurs youth coaches were so impressed with his performance that they invited him to join their academy. Harry excitedly said, "Yes please!" – and the rest is football history.

Well, actually the story isn't quite that simple. Harry didn't just glide through the Tottenham youth teams like one of his super-accurate shots. No, in order to become Spurs' star striker and England captain, he had to show real determination and resilience to overcome setbacks along the way.

Harry often found it hard to stand out at the Spurs academy because there were so many other gifted young players at the club. In the end, it wasn't just Harry's footballing talent that took him through into the Tottenham first team; it was also his never-give-up attitude. He believed in his own ability and knew that if he worked hard enough, he would achieve his dream eventually.

When Spurs were thinking about letting him leave at the age of fourteen Harry signed up for exhausting extra sessions with a fitness coach to improve his sprint speed. After that, they asked him to stay.

When he seemed to be stuck just outside the Tottenham first team at the age of seventeen, Harry remained behind after training for extra shooting sessions with **Jermain Defoe** to improve his accuracy and his confidence in front of goal. He learned to strike the ball early, to react positively after each miss and also to picture exactly where he wanted his shot to end up.

But despite all his hard work, Spurs still didn't think that Harry was ready for the Premier League yet. So they sent him away to gain experience in the lower leagues. He didn't just go out on loan once, though; he left Tottenham *four* times, to join four different clubs: Leyton Orient in League One, then Millwall in the Championship, then Norwich City in the Premier League, and finally, back to the Championship to play for Leicester City.

Sometimes Harry started a match, but often he found himself sitting on the bench. Those were tough and uncertain times, filled with frustration and doubts. If he wasn't playing regularly for Leicester or Norwich, how was he going to get into the Spurs team? Was he *really* good enough? What if Tottenham didn't want him back? What if, despite giving everything, his dream of being a top Premier League striker didn't come true?

But through it all, Harry continued to believe in himself.

The disappointments were all part of the learning process and there was no way that he was going to give up now. Eventually, he would achieve his long-term goal. Until then, he just had to stay strong and keep working towards that target, one goal at a time...

Halfway through the 2013–14 season, Tottenham changed their manager and Harry finally got his chance in the first team. On 7 April, he started his first Premier League match for Spurs, at home against Sunderland. "Come on!" he thought to himself. He was fired up and ready to score. All those setbacks and disappointments earlier in his football career had only made him more determined to become a superstar striker, for Tottenham and for England. It was time to achieve his Premier League goals.

As he walked out at White Hart Lane that day, Harry felt full of confidence. Before kick-off, he had gone through different images in his head of exactly how he was going to score – a tap-in at the front post, a header at the back post, a one-on-one with the keeper. To make the visualization more realistic, he had even thought about little details like what colour kit his opponents would be wearing and how long the grass would be. That was all part of his preparation for becoming Tottenham's big-game player.

*GOAL!* against Sunderland ...

*GOAL!* against West Brom ...

*GOAL!* against Fulham.

Three in three – a new Premier League hero was born.

Ahead of the 2014–15 season, Harry set himself the target of scoring fifteen goals. That seemed ambitious, but by December, he had to raise it to twenty, and by February, he had to raise it again to thirty. Now that he'd found his top form, he just couldn't stop scoring. He finished with thirty-one goals in all competitions – not bad for a twenty-year-old in his breakthrough year!

Soon, Harry was a national hero too. In fact, by the time England travelled to Russia for the 2018 World Cup, he was the team captain, as well as their star striker. The whole country was counting on him to lead England to victory. But with three minutes to go in their first group game against Tunisia, England were heading for a disappointing 1–1 draw. Not good enough! They needed to start the World Cup with a win.

The pressure was building with every single second. England were playing in front of over 40,000 fans in the Volgograd Arena, plus there were millions more watching at home on TV. Harry was determined not to let his nation down.

"Come on, there's still time to score the winner," he kept telling himself.

As **Kieran Trippier** curled one last corner kick into the box, Harry cleverly snuck into space at the back post and then waited. It was like he knew exactly where the flick-on would land. With a cool, calm swivel of his head, Harry knocked home the winning goal for England.

Now that's what we call a smart football hero!

# SO ARE YOU READY TO THINK SMART?

As you've seen in this section, you can't always control what happens on the pitch. You can't help it if your goalkeeper flaps at an easy save and the ball skids in. You can't help it if your striker fluffs an easy chance. But you can control how you react to what happens on the pitch.

Your mind is your most powerful tool.

And when you train that tool, it helps your body to play at its best.

Mindset beats talent. Thinking smart is what separates the very best footballers from the good footballers. And now you know how to do it too.

Here's your challenge: think about what can be gained, not what could be lost. Always say do, never say don't. Act like you're the best player, then maybe eventually you will be. Tell yourself you can and you're halfway there.

It isn't possible to play at your best all of the time. It isn't possible to feel happy all of the time. There will be games where you don't feel as confident. There will be times when you aren't as motivated. But using these tricks can help you to bounce back with confidence, step out of your comfort zone and set you on the path to success!

# TOP TEN TIPS FOR THINKING SMART:

1. Focus on what you would like to happen.

2. Believe you can.

3. Everybody fails. Everybody has disappointments. Sometimes you need to take one step back to take two steps forward. Embrace the power of persistence!

4. It's not how good you are. It's how good you can be.

5. Always remember the power of "yet".

6. Reflect on your wins and losses and ask yourself why they happened. Then focus on the next challenge.

7. Control what you can. Don't worry about what you can't control.

8. Always look for challenges. They are an opportunity to shine, not a chance to fail.

9. Be brave! Nobody ever won the World Cup or the Champions League without stepping out of their comfort zone.

10. You play football because it is fun. Enjoy the experience.

# ULTIMATE CHALLENGES TO THINK SMART:

1. Next month, revisit those goals you wrote down. Have you got any closer to any, or maybe even achieved some? Good. It's time to write down a new set of short-term goals. Make sure that they challenge you. Goal-setting is a constant process, which means you need to keep on rewriting those goals as you get better.

2. Watch your favourite footballer and see how they move on a football pitch. Do they have a great big smile? Do they make their body as big as possible and puff their chest out? If so, try copying the way they move.

3. Film yourself playing or training. When you've done a skill really well, watch that skill back before big games to build your confidence.

4. Practise your skills in pressure situations. It could be a game of FIFA against your friend where the loser has to buy the winner a packet of sweets, or maybe a keepy-uppie competition where you're allowed to boo each other. Keep track of who wins each time.

5. Remember your best performances and write down why they were so good. Make them as real as possible. You've done it before so you can do it again – and even better next time!

# FINE-TUNE YOUR PERFORMANCES

Your body is like a racing car. On its best days it zooms around the football pitch at maximum speed, weaving in and out of opponents as if they weren't there. But think about all that goes into a racing car's optimal performance. It needs the right fuel. Mechanics tinker with the engine to keep it in perfect condition. Specific tyres are chosen for the racetrack and the conditions.

If the car isn't looked after between races, it won't be able to perform at its best on competition day. Maybe there's a screw loose but the mechanics don't bother checking. Perhaps the dozy driver puts in the wrong fuel. The flag waves, the cars are off ... only this one is already sputtering. The driver tries to keep going but it breaks down before it finishes the race.

But how does all this help you to become a better footballer? Well, just like a racing car, your body needs fuel. Only, the fuel your body needs isn't petrol.

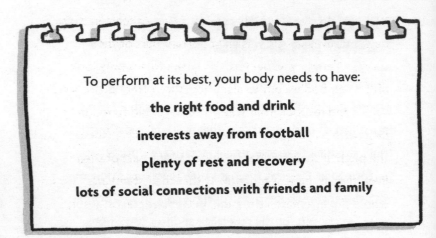

To perform at its best, your body needs to have:

**the right food and drink**

**interests away from football**

**plenty of rest and recovery**

**lots of social connections with friends and family**

The way you live when you aren't playing football directly impacts how you play football. You need to take care of your body and your mind when you are off the pitch. That way, your mind and body will take care of you when you are on the pitch.

As **Sir Alex Ferguson** said: "If you can assemble a team of eleven talented players who concentrate intently during training sessions, take care of their diet and bodies, get enough sleep and show up on time, then you are almost halfway to winning a trophy."

And Sir Alex knows what he's talking about, having won a trophy or two – or forty-six, to be precise, including the Champions League (twice!), the Premier League (thirteen times!) and the FA Cup (five times!).

Yes, Manchester United had a very talented team in those days, but living smart was an important part of their success. Ferguson expected his players to not only look after their bodies, but to also show the correct attitudes, values and respect. That way his teams could function best, with players who always tried their best on and off the pitch. If their standards slipped in any part of their lives, then it made it more likely that their standards would slip in a match situation. Better people, Ferguson believed, make better footballers.

So, would you like to learn the secrets of living smart? Let's get started.

# 01 LIVE LIKE ARSENAL'S INVINCIBLES
## BE NICE TO YOUR BODY

## ARSENAL FC

**NICKNAME:** the Gunners

**FOUNDED IN:** 1886, Woolwich, London

**(TEAM) HERO MOMENT:** winning the Premier League in 2004 without losing a single match

Food: we all eat it. That's because food is made up of nutrients that give us lots of energy, help us to grow and keep us healthy. All of which are important, especially if we're racing around a football pitch for ninety minutes.

But what should we eat and when? These days, all the top teams have specially-trained chefs and nutritionists to give them all the answers, but it wasn't like that in the early days of the Premier League. No, back then, no one seemed to understand the importance of a healthy, balanced diet, and so players were often free to eat whatever they liked. Do you know what they call that? A recipe for disaster! (Geddit?)

When Dutch striker **Dennis Bergkamp** arrived at Arsenal in 1995, he was shocked by what he saw on his team-mates' plates: "In my first season the pre-match meal would be white beans in tomato sauce [that's baked beans by the way!], bacon, scrambled eggs... And on the coach the other players would be eating crisps and chocolate."

Now, some of you might be thinking, "Yum, yes please! What's wrong with that?", so let's get a little bit sciency here.

Different foods are full of various nutrients, which help your body in lots of amazing ways. Some foods only have small nutritional benefits, while others have such amazing benefits that they are called **superfoods**. You may have heard the old tale that eating carrots will help you to see at night. Unfortunately, that's not quite true, but carrots do contain vitamin A, which helps your eyesight to stay in top condition.

All fruit and vegetables are packed full of **vitamins and minerals** that help to protect your body from disease and keep it working at its best. That's why you should always aim to eat at least five portions of fruit and veg a day. However, vitamins and minerals are just two types of nutrients found in food and drink.

The main nutrients we get from our food are carbohydrates, fats and protein.

- **Carbohydrates** provide energy to the body. Foods high in carbohydrates include cereal, pasta, rice and potatoes.
- **Fats** also provide energy (but not as much as carbohydrates) and keep the body warm. There are good fats (yay!) and not-so-good fats (boo!). Foods high in good fats include nuts, fish and avocados. Foods high in not-so-good fats include butter, chocolate and crisps.
- **Protein** helps the body to grow and repair itself. Foods high in protein include eggs, beans and meat.

## BALANCE YOUR PLATE

OK, so what do we think of that Arsenal pre-match meal now? Bacon, eggs, beans, chocolate, crisps – hmmmm sounds like lots of protein and lots of fats, doesn't it? And not the good kind! High-fat meals will slow you down, which is a spectacularly bad idea if your job is to run around a big, long football pitch for ninety minutes.

No wonder Bergkamp didn't want to join in! From his time at top Italian club Inter Milan, he already understood the link between food and performance. As he said, "The better your body is prepared, the better you can do your work." So, instead of filling up on fatty fried breakfasts, he wanted to eat meals that gave him extra energy, including important carbohydrates like pasta.

143

You see, all meals for a footballer should include all three types of nutrients, which helps you to have a balanced diet. A balanced diet is one that includes all the nutrients your body needs. This means around 55% of energy from carbohydrates, 25% from fat and 20% from proteins.

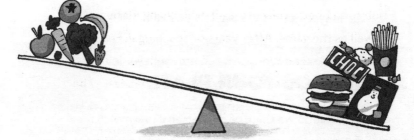

However, everyone has a different body that has different requirements. Some people may need more proteins, while others might need less fat.

The best way to have a balanced diet is by having three balanced meals each day: breakfast, lunch and dinner. Any less than three meals and there's danger that you'll top up your diet with sugary snacks like biscuits.

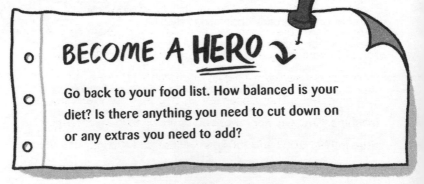

## BECOME A HERO

Go back to your food list. How balanced is your diet? Is there anything you need to cut down on or any extras you need to add?

It's fine to have the odd treat, but too many treats will lead to an unbalanced diet that will give you less energy on the pitch, cause your body to take longer to recover after exercise and increase the risk of injury.

So, back to that unbalanced bunch at Arsenal. Luckily, the club soon hired a new manager, who changed the menu, as well as the game. After years of coaching in France and Japan, **Arsène Wenger** was a firm believer in healthy living and healthy eating. So, as soon as he arrived, Wenger banned all chocolate bars and burgers, and changed the pre-match meal to plain, boiled chicken with vegetables and no sauce. As you can imagine, all the Arsenal players were furious, even Bergkamp: "I mean, I like a bit of flavour, and, really, this was no fun."

Sounds fussy, doesn't he? But in the end, the club found that beautiful thing: balance. By stirring in a tasty sauce, Arsenal were able to serve up the right food for success – full of flavour as well as nutrients. Much better! And once their players were both happy and healthy, there was no stopping them. They became a fit, strong, trophy-winning machine. "The Gunners" went on to lift three Premier League titles in 1998, 2002 *and* 2004, as well as four FA Cups.

**Arsenal's "Invincibles"** even played the whole of the 2003–04 season without losing a single league game. Let's hope they celebrated that achievement with something better than boiled chicken!

Anyway, the message of this story? Eat well, win well! Wenger's nutrition revolution has led to every top club hiring their own nutritionists, with some players even having their own personal nutritionists and chefs.

# THIRSTY WORK

Did you know that over half of your body is water? Look at your hands. There are five fingers, right? Now imagine three of those just being water. No skin, no bone, just liquid. That's the ratio of water in your body – and there's even more in your brain (around 73%)! It's as if you're hauling around a whole swimming pool in your body every day.

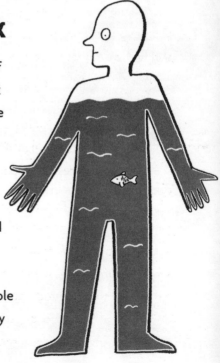

Water plays an important role in your body. Water:

- transports nutrients
- keeps our bodies at the right temperature
- helps our blood pressure
- removes waste products (that's poo and wee)
- aids breathing

When you play football, you lose water through sweat, which helps to keep our bodies at the right temperature. If you lose too much water, then you become dehydrated, and when you're dehydrated, your mental and physical abilities all decline. You get a headache or a fuzzy head and find it's harder to concentrate and that your decision-

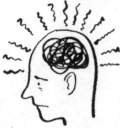

making gets worse. You become weaker and you can't run for long periods of time. Even losing as little as 2% of your body weight from dehydration will have a negative impact on your performance.

Drinking plenty of liquids throughout the day helps to prevent dehydration. OK, sounds simple, but what should we drink and when? Well, before Wenger came along, Arsenal had the wrong answer for that one too: lots of sugary, fizzy drinks and alcohol too. But don't worry, the French manager soon put things right, banning all liquids except water! Yes, that's what footballers need to drink lots of, before a game, at half-time and also after a game to make sure they always have enough in their bodies.

There's an easy way to tell how hydrated you are.

Can you guess what it is?

It's really simple and even more gross...

**[Drum roll, please.]**

It's by checking the colour of your wee!

If your wee is the colour of water, then that means you're nice and hydrated. You're perfectly set to play at your maximum ability, with full concentration, strength and power. But the darker your wee, the more dehydrated you are. If it comes out brown, then you really do need to drink something quickly!

## MATCH DAY

Before a game, footballers need to have nice, clear wee and plenty of energy from food high in carbohydrates. Southampton star **Nathan Redmond** (Matt said we had to include at least one Saints hero in the book) has scrambled eggs on toast before a match, while former England captain **Wayne Rooney** likes chocolate cereal and a banana.

Both meals have loads of slow-release carbohydrates, which means that the players will still have plenty of energy in the final ten minutes.

After a game, it's then important to have lots of protein so that your muscles can repair themselves quickly and carry on growing. An ideal meal might be something like grilled fish or chilli con carne, but many footballers use the time after a game to treat themselves with their favourite foods such as pizza or a naughty Nando's. Remember, as long as it's done in moderation (no more than 20% of your total food), then it is fine to have a treat every now and again!

## BECOME A HERO

To make the most of nutrition, experiment with different balanced meals before and after a match. Make sure you get enough fats, carbohydrates and proteins – not to mention fruits, vegetables, water, and don't forget flavour – so that you feel fit, strong, and as invincible as Wenger's Arsenal team.

So, be nice to your body and it'll be nice to you. But as you're about to see, you don't just need food and drink to live smart.

# 02 LIVE LIKE ALUKO
## FEED YOUR BRAIN

## ENI ALUKO

**NATIONALITY:** English

**POSITION:** Forward

**HERO MOMENT:** earning a whopping 102 caps for England (and scoring thirty-three goals)

As we learned in the Think Smart section, your brain has to work hard when you play football. To make sure that it is as sharp as possible when it matters most, it's important to feed your brain away from the football pitch too.

But how can you feed a brain? We don't mean with food. Instead, we mean with knowledge.

This knowledge doesn't have to be football knowledge. In fact, it's probably better if your brain isn't always fed football knowledge. That's because it's important to develop interests away from football. Portuguese midfielder, **Bernardo Silva**, for example, plays the piano. Spanish right-back **Héctor Bellerín** runs his own advertising agency. US legend **Alex Morgan** writes her own series of children's books. Manchester United's **Marcus Rashford** helps a charity called FareShare in their bid to reduce food poverty.

And for another England striker, **Eni Aluko**, the interests she developed away from football helped her to become so good at football that she not only played for Chelsea and Juventus, but also for England!

Growing up in Birmingham, Aluko loved playing football with her family and friends, but for a long time, she couldn't see a way to make it her full-time professional career. How would she earn enough money? Instead of giving up on football, she decided to follow two dreams at the same time.

While she was scoring the winner for Charlton Athletic in the 2005 FA Women's Cup Final, she was also studying hard for her A-levels.

And while she was playing for England at the 2007 World Cup, she was also acing her way to a first-class degree in Law at Brunel University.

Becoming a lawyer had always been Aluko's second dream job, ever since she read Harper Lee's book *To Kill a Mockingbird* at school. Atticus Finch, the lawyer in the story, was so brave and determined to fight for justice. Aluko decided that was what she wanted to do too.

But to be a lawyer and a top footballer at the same time? Surely, you've got to be some kind of superhero! Aluko admitted that "... it wasn't always easy to juggle my [football] dreams alongside my education". But by planning her days carefully and making the most of her time, she managed it.

It was only in 2015 that Aluko focused fully on football. She went on to win three league titles with Chelsea and another at Juventus, before retiring in 2020. So, what next – a long, illustrious law career? Not for now, but her studies will come in useful as the first-ever sporting director of National Women's Soccer League side Angel City in the US.

# RELAX!

We know studying hard might not sound like the best way to unwind after a tough game of football, but actually Aluko found it helpful: "It was refreshing to have friends outside of that bubble, and to have purpose and energy invested beyond winning trophies or tournaments," she said.

Taking your mind off football every now and again helps you to relax and refocus. We both love football, but thinking about it 24/7 would drive us crazy! There's nothing worse than playing poorly and losing a game and replaying it over and over in your mind until the next time you get to finally step onto a pitch. This would increase

the chances of stress, which has all sorts of negative impacts on physical and mental health. At its worst, it could even lead to burnout, which is every bit as scary as it sounds.

As Dutch legend **Wesley Sneijder** said: "You can't play at your top level every week if you're always thinking about football."

Instead, the world's best players assess how they played, decide what they will do to improve their performance next time around, and then they stop thinking about football. This helps to reduce their stress levels and means that they can play the next match with full focus, motivation and commitment. They also enjoy football more as a result.

Often, these other interests are transferable skills that improve your ability to play football. Studying helped Aluko improve her concentration and focus, which made it easier for her to take on the tactics and strategies that her coaches asked of her. Playing the piano like **Silva** inspires creativity and improves attention span – skills that can bring rewards on the pitch. Running a business like **Bellerín** develops leadership. Working with charities like **Rashford** keeps you humble and builds your social network, giving you important attitudes and values to take into a game.

## BECOME A HERO ↴

What have you always wanted to do (other than become a football star, obviously!)? Why not give it a go? Simply trying it out will help your football skills by keeping your brain nice and fresh for when it matters on the pitch. Plus, it's always nice to step out of your comfort zone and learn new skills!

## INSPIRATIONAL STUFF

Feeding your brain with non-football knowledge is important. But it's also nice to feed it plenty of football knowledge. One of the best ways to do that is by reading books and stories about football and footballers (you've made a great start by reading this one!).

When you read Aluko's story, did it inspire you?

Reading stories of how footballers got to where they are isn't only useful in inspiring you, but also in giving you helpful pointers and ideas. Reading former Wimbledon hardman **Vinnie Jones**'s autobiography inspired Seth to set himself a goal of playing football in a foreign country. He wrote to hundreds of teams in Europe and ended up playing professionally in both Brazil and Sri Lanka! Without reading Vinnie's story, that may never have happened.

You'd be surprised by how many footballers were once just like you. They lived in houses just like yours, went to school just like you and ate the same kind of food as you do.

Take Danish keeper **Kasper Schmeichel** (remember his father, Peter, from the transferable skills section?). He loved learning about other footballers' stories. He'd spend hours searching YouTube to see his heroes in action. He'd watch how they performed and then try to copy it in his own training sessions.

The Internet is full of great stories and ideas that you can use to improve your own game. You can watch videos of your heroes in action, read articles, view documentaries and use social media to learn new ideas. Each of those will feed your brain and keep it running at its maximum for when it counts.

And those books and stories don't even need to be about footballers! Premier League full-back **Joe Bryan** loves reading about the life stories of inspirational people. His favourite books include *Legacy* by James Kerr as well as engineer Elon Musk's autobiography. "If you can take messages out of the books and take advice it'll improve you as a person and a player," he said. "You want a book to make you question some of the things you do in your life and see if you can improve."

That's exactly the impact that reading *To Kill a Mockingbird* had on Aluko. She came away with a new sense of purpose that continues to this day: "I wanted to confront injustice, to defend those who couldn't defend themselves..."

## BECOME A HERO

Write down five things that you've read so far in this book that you can put into practice in your life. Which other books and stories do you think may give you good advice to help you improve?

Learning new stuff isn't the only way to improve and feed your brain. There's something else that's vitally important. And the good news is that you already do it. In fact, you've probably done it so much that it's taken up around a third of your life.

Have you guessed what it is yet?

Here's a clue: zzzzZZZ.

# 03 LIVE LIKE AGÜERO
## GET THE RIGHT REST AND RECOVERY

## SERGIO AGÜERO

**NATIONALITY:** Argentinian

**POSITION:** Forward

**HERO MOMENT:** scoring a last-minute goal in 2012 to give City their first top division title in forty-four years

When was the last time you played in a really tough football match? Do you remember how tired your body felt at the final whistle? Your brain and muscles had been working hard since kick-off and by the end of the game you felt drained of energy.

Well, that was how super striker **Sergio Agüero** was feeling at the start of the 2014–15 Premier League season. Most years, he felt much fresher after a holiday in the sun, but this summer, he'd been busy helping Argentina go all the way to the World Cup final in Brazil. Back at Manchester City, he was still scoring goals – I mean, when doesn't he? – but he definitely didn't seem his usual self.

As we've already learned, you can recharge your energy supplies with the right food and drink. After a trip to the doctor, Agüero switched to a more balanced diet, but what he also really needed was rest. You see, if you keep playing lots and lots of football, before your energy supplies have recovered, you may end up damaging your body by overtraining. This is because your body is only capable of doing so much.

The time when you recover after a match or training session is when you actually make your biggest improvements. Without the right amount of rest and recovery, you won't be able to get fitter and stronger.

# REST UP

But with the right amount of rest and recovery, you can play and train at your best. So, what did Agüero have to do – sit still for hours and hours? Not necessarily. Resting can involve anything that means you don't move around that much. A rest period can be a great time to learn a new skill or pursue a (low-intensity) new passion. Or, if you really want to relax, then just watching a film, reading a book or playing video games are also fantastic ways to switch off.

But recovery doesn't have to mean doing nothing. While passive recovery involves resting, *active* recovery is easy exercise such as a gentle bicycle ride, a yoga session or a walk around the block. This easy exercise increases the blood flow to your tired muscles, which feeds them oxygen and helps them recover more quickly.

Everybody is different and has their own recovery routine, but many footballers favour passive recovery after a game, followed by active recovery the next morning. Once their bodies are back to the top of their game, they can start training at full speed.

Agüero got as much rest as he could after training, but he still didn't feel as sharp as he normally did on the football pitch. That's because he was missing the most important ingredient in any footballer's recovery plan: a good night's sleep!

# FORTY WINKS

While you're tucked under your duvet with your head buried into your pillow, dreaming of scoring the winner at Wembley (everyone dreams about that, right?), amazing things happen to your body.

Let's start with the physical changes that occur when you sleep:

- Human growth hormone (HGH) is released. This repairs cells, boosts muscle growth and strength and helps your body to grow.
- Your immune system refreshes, which helps you to fight off sickness and infection.
- Your appetite is regulated, which means you feel the right level of hungry the next day. This makes you less likely to eat sugary snacks and junk food when you wake up.
- Muscle energy stores increase quicker.
- Your heart gets a nice rest after spending the day working hard pumping blood all around your body. This reduces the risk of heart disease and keeps blood pressure low.

Now for the mental changes:

- Neural connections in your brain – which control everything in your body – actually strengthen overnight. This improves your memory, which means that the skills you learn are more likely to stick.
- Brain circuits are repaired, which helps you to control your emotions, reduces stress and improves mood.
- When you wake up from a nice, long sleep, you feel super alert. Because of the rest your brain has had, you're able to concentrate for the whole day! This is especially important for elite footballers, who have to make split-second decisions on the pitch.

And when you don't sleep enough, the opposite happens. You become more irritable and forgetful. You can't concentrate well and make wrong decisions. You lose energy quicker. You become ill and get injured more often.

 So make sure you get plenty of sleep. Although everybody is different, the general rule is that the younger you are, the more sleep you need. So newborn babies may sleep as much as seventeen hours a day, whereas adults need between seven and nine hours. Seven-year-olds need between ten and eleven hours while fourteen-year-olds need nine hours.

Sleep expert Matthew Walker says that sleeping less than six hours a night has drastic results for athletes. These include becoming physically exhausted 10–30% more quickly, being able to jump much lower and even having less ability to sweat.

So, back to Agüero, who wasn't sleeping well, and wasn't sleeping enough. Naturally, he liked to go to bed late and wake up late, but he couldn't do that because he had to get up early every morning to go to training. So, how could he make sure that he was still getting the right amount of rest and recovery?

Agüero decided to speak to a world-famous sleep coach (yes, that's a real job, we promise!) called Nick Littlehales and ask for his help.

After watching him sleep, Littlehales gave him lots of amazing advice, including:

1. Change your sleeping position.
2. Get a much better mattress (designed especially for Agüero's height and weight).
3. Start taking an afternoon nap.

And just like that, all of Agüero's sleeping and scoring problems were solved! On the morning of the next match day, he woke up feeling fresh and ready to shine. Manchester City thrashed Tottenham 4–1 and Agüero grabbed all four goals. So, you there you have it – the power of a good night's sleep!

And Agüero's not the only footballer who values rest and recovery. Atlético Madrid's midfielder **Marcos Llorente** even bought a £30,000 bed that scientists say slows down the ageing process!

# BECOME A HERO ↘

If you don't have lots of money to spend on a brand-new bed, don't worry! There are lots of other ways you can make sure you get all of the benefits of sleep. Tonight, when you head up to your bedroom, try the following and see how much better you sleep:

- **Stick to a good sleep schedule.**

This will help you to get the right amount of sleep. A good sleep schedule means going to bed at the same time every night and waking up at the same time every morning. So, to get nine hours on a school night, for example, your schedule could be to sleep from 10 p.m. until 7 a.m. Eventually, your body will adapt so that it feels tired when it's time to go to bed and wakes up without an alarm clock!

- **Get a good bedtime routine.**

If you do the same things in the same order every night (put on your pyjamas, brush your teeth, read a few chapters of your book), that helps your brain get ready for bed too.

- **Turn off your technology.**

Phones, iPads and games consoles are the enemies of good sleep. Their screens emit blue light, which messes with your circadian rhythms (a really fancy name for your body clock, which tells you when you feel tired). An hour before it's time to sleep, it's best to put the games console away and pick a relaxing activity, such as reading a book, listening to a podcast or, our personal favourite, naming as many footballers as we can (it's like counting sheep, only way better).

- **Get your room right.**

Keeping the room as dark as possible and cool helps your body to fall asleep quicker and wake up feeling refreshed.

As the story of Agüero shows, when you sleep well, recover well, eat well, feed your brain and stay hydrated, you'll be in good condition to train and play at your best. Your body will feel at full power. But as we're about to find out, there's another way to unlock the full power of your mind, just like Leicester City did in 2016.

# 04

## LIVE LIKE LEICESTER'S UNBELIEVABLES
## TEAMWORK MAKES THE DREAM WORK!

# LEICESTER CITY FC

**NICKNAME:** the Foxes

**FOUNDED IN:** 1884, Fosse Way, Leicester

**(TEAM) HERO MOMENT:** winning the Premier League title in 2016, despite being favourites for relegation at the start of the season

No footballer has ever got to where they are by themselves. Even Messi and Miedema would struggle to win a game of football all on their own. They need at least a few team-mates around to give them a chance.

And to become a professional footballer in the first place, you need far more than just team-mates. There's a long list of thank you letters to write:

- to the family and friends who put up with constant kick-arounds and your bad moods when you've lost, and who always cheered you on from the sidelines, no matter what the weather and how far they had to travel
- to the local football club coaches who taught you about the game and encouraged you to enjoy it
- to the scouts who spotted your talent and gave you a chance
- to the academy coaches who believed in you and showed you ways to become a better player
- to the physios and doctors who helped keep you fit and injury-free
- to the psychologists who worked on building your winning mindset
- to the personal chefs, trainers, sleep coaches and private jet pilots (hey, we can all dream, can't we?!)
- and, of course, to every player and manager you've ever played with or for

Together, we call these properly awesome people the **support network**. That's because they help a footballer to perform at their best.

Let's look at some examples from our football heroes:

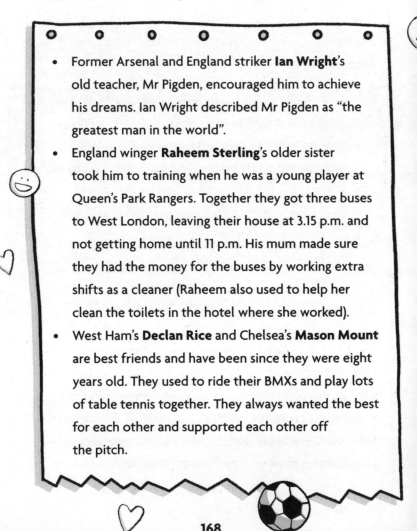

- Former Arsenal and England striker **Ian Wright**'s old teacher, Mr Pigden, encouraged him to achieve his dreams. Ian Wright described Mr Pigden as "the greatest man in the world".

- England winger **Raheem Sterling**'s older sister took him to training when he was a young player at Queen's Park Rangers. Together they got three buses to West London, leaving their house at 3.15 p.m. and not getting home until 11 p.m. His mum made sure they had the money for the buses by working extra shifts as a cleaner (Raheem also used to help her clean the toilets in the hotel where she worked).

- West Ham's **Declan Rice** and Chelsea's **Mason Mount** are best friends and have been since they were eight years old. They used to ride their BMXs and play lots of table tennis together. They always wanted the best for each other and supported each other off the pitch.

- Chelsea and England star **Fran Kirby** was struck by grief at the age of fourteen after the death of her mum. She relied on her friends to help her and even stopped playing football for four years. Jules Townrow, the physiotherapist at the club Kirby started playing for, Reading, invited her round to watch TV, eat pizza and just chat. Then, after a while, Fran's best friend, Sarah Devern, asked her to come and play for her Sunday league team. Fran did, enjoyed it, and was soon back playing for Reading. She went on to sign a professional contract with Reading and to play for England.

None of our heroes would have achieved as much without their support networks. A support network encourages you to achieve your goals, celebrates your successes and picks you up after a setback. Your network pushes you to be the best you can be. Most importantly, it keeps you mentally well, which helps to prevent feelings of loneliness.

Spending time with friends and family makes you feel happy, confident, gives you a purpose and reduces stress. It could be playing football together or doing activities that help you to switch off from football, such as skateboarding, playing video games or even just hanging out.

## FRIENDS OF INFLUENCE

Your thoughts and actions are influenced by the people you surround yourself with. Former Arsenal and Manchester United striker **Robin van Persie** said that every single person he knew had an impact on his life. To be the best he could be, he needed those people to have a positive impact. He knew how important it is to have a strong support network.

Friends who laugh at you for training hard and who encourage you to skip football sessions have a bad effect. They would form a weak support network. However, friends that encourage you (just like Mason and Declan encouraged each other) can help you to achieve your goals. They train alongside you, give you tips that they've learned from their own experiences and help you to improve your weaknesses. It's no coincidence that Mason and Declan *both* became professional footballers (even though Declan was released by Chelsea at the age of fourteen) and *both* now play for England. Friends like these, and support networks like these, keep you grounded in victory and lift your spirits in defeat.

When you become friends with your team-mates, amazing things can happen on the football pitch. Take Leicester City, for example. Ahead of the 2015–16 season, they were favourites to be relegated from the Premier League. The odds of them lifting the title? 5,000–1!

But what the rest of the Premier League hadn't realized yet was that Leicester City were becoming an unbeatable band of football brothers. The more the players talked off the pitch, the stronger the team spirit grew. They had lots in common, especially when it came to setbacks suffered earlier in their careers.

**Danny Drinkwater** had been rejected by his boyhood club Manchester United, and the same had happened to **Jamie Vardy** at Sheffield Wednesday and **Kasper Schmeichel** at Manchester City. **Riyad Mahrez** had been told that he was too small to become a pro and so had **N'Golo Kanté**. But each of them had bounced back to prove people wrong; now, it was time to pull off something truly unbelievable together.

After ten games, the Foxes were fifth in the table.

After twenty, they sat second behind Arsenal.

And after thirty-eight, they were crowned the new Premier League champions!

Unbelievable! So, how did Leicester do it? Well, it certainly helped that they had some high-quality stars and a clear game plan, but it was also because of their special team bond. They won together and had fun together. As Schmeichel said, "Our team spirit is great, we do a lot of things together and always have done…"

When Leicester kept their first clean sheet of the season, their Italian manager, **Claudio Ranieri**, treated his whole team to pizzas. There was only one catch: they had to make them together first!

At Christmas, the squad all dressed up as superheroes for a special night out in Copenhagen. There was a Power

Ranger, a Spider-Man, a Batman (**Robert Huth**, in case you wondered) and all four Teenage Mutant Ninja Turtles!

At Easter, **Christian Fuchs** challenged Vardy to a game of Russian egg roulette. Basically, they splatted eggs on each other's heads until one of them cracked. (Geddit?)

All that fun off the pitch definitely paid off on the pitch for Leicester. The players knew and understood each other really well, which helped them work together towards their unbelievable achievement of becoming Premier League champions.

# BECOME A HERO ↘

How can you bring other people on by being part of their support network? Write down the names of three people and come up with three ideas of how you could help them play at their best.

As Leicester City proved, it's important to spend time with your support network. Remember, it isn't just their job to support you but also your job to support them. After all, everyone needs support when learning new skills. Babies need to be picked up by their parents when they're learning to walk. And even the world's very best footballers need others to help them along the way.

# 05 LIVE LIKE SON
## SHOW RESPECT

# SON HEUNG-MIN

**NATIONALITY:** South Korean

**POSITION:** Forward

**HERO MOMENT:** being named Best Footballer
in Asia five times — and counting!

The last time you went on a school trip we bet you got the usual talking-to beforehand in assembly. "It's really important that you behave well because you are representing the school. Be polite. Respect those around you. Blah, blah, blah." When you then went on the trip to the museum or the activity centre or – if you were really lucky – the football stadium, you made sure you listened and didn't mess around. The next day in assembly, your teachers told you how proud they were of you all and how well it reflected on the school.

The same is true in football.

The better you behave in training sessions and games, the more likely you are to succeed both as part of a team and as an individual.

It's time for another story.

# *Football Fairy Tale:*
## The Player Who Impressed

Once upon a time, **Danny Welbeck** was a young striker in the Manchester United academy when Sir Alex Ferguson first met him. What impressed Ferguson most was not Welbeck's ability on the pitch, but the way he showed respect. At the end of every training session Welbeck would collect the balls in for the coach. That small action was enough to show Ferguson that he should keep working on Welbeck.

And what happened to Danny? Well, he played for the Manchester United senior team. And then England. THE END.

Football coaches look for every small clue about who will become a good player. Welbeck's dedication and humility in collecting the balls proved that he was willing to work at his game. He would be dedicated in training and wouldn't become arrogant. He was also someone who helped others, showing that he'd be a top team player.

# QUIZ TIME

**You are a scout for young talent. Which player are you most likely to choose for a contract?**

**Player A:** Arrives early. Smiles and shakes hands with the coaches and other club staff. Says "hello" to other trialists. Looks smart in their shirt and tie. Listens to instructions. Helps to carry equipment. Has cleaned their own boots that morning. Wears their training shirt tucked in. Asks helpful questions. Takes responsibility for their own equipment.

**Player B:** Turns up late. Their parents are carrying their sports bag. They are dressed inappropriately. Their boots still have last week's mud on them. Doesn't greet the coaches. Doesn't help to carry the equipment to the training field or collect it at the end. Messes around while the coach is speaking. Disappears immediately after the session.

The answer? It's Player A of course! Their actions suggest they are keen to learn and will represent the club in the right way. They take responsibility for their own actions, which means they are likely to work hard and smart when they're at home. What about Player B? Well, their bad manners and selfish attitude suggest they are not a team player. If they are introduced to the team, there could be trouble – no matter how good they are!

One player with an attitude to admire (he's definitely Player A) is Tottenham forward **Son Heung-min**. Even though he's now one of the Premier League's greatest players as well as one of South Korea's most famous celebrities, he has stayed humble and dedicated to his sport. He's a great example of what you can achieve with a polite, positive attitude.

Son's old Hamburg manager, **Thorsten Fink**, noticed it straight away: "He was a hard worker and, after training, he'd do extra training on his own. He was honest, he listened, he was never late, and his discipline was really impressive."

Yes, Son is the perfect pro. He always gives 110% effort on the pitch, and never tires of posing for selfie photos with the fans afterwards. He plays the game with a permanent smile on his face, grateful for every opportunity. Everyone at Tottenham feeds off his energy, but especially the players, who each have their own special handshake with Son. When he won all four of his club's end-of-season awards in 2020 for the second year in a row, he remembered to thank not only his supporters and team-mates, but also all the staff at the club (part of his support network!). What a thoughtful guy!

Son says that he gets it from his dad, Son Woong-jung, who coached him when he was a kid and taught him all about respect: "My father told me when I was young that if I was through on goal but an opponent fell and hurt themselves, I should put the ball out and check on the opponent. Because if you're a good footballer but don't know how to respect others, you're nobody."

Well said, Son! We couldn't agree more. There's a famous saying that "Talent gets you in the room, but your attitude keeps you in the room". By following Son's advice and the tips below, you can give yourself the best chance possible of "staying in the room".

# BECOME A HERO ↴

## A PRO'S GUIDE TO SHOWING RESPECT IN TEN EASY STEPS

1. Always arrive early. It shows that you are reliable.

2. Dress smartly to play smartly. It gives a good first impression and shows you take pride in yourself.

3. Say "hello" to every one of your team-mates and the coach. It helps to build relationships.

4. When a coach is speaking, stop what you're doing and listen. Watch their eyes to show you are taking in every word. It suggests you are going to take in their advice and use it in the right way.

5. Mind your "P"s and "Q"s – which is a weird way of saying, "Be polite by saying please and thank you." Doing the small things well shows you are likely to do the big things well too.

6. Take responsibility for your own equipment. Clean your boots after each game and pack your own bag. It shows you want to take control.

7. Shake hands with the referee and opponents after a game. It proves you are mature and respect those around you.

8. Always stay positive and support those around you – even if you're dropped to the bench. It shows you are kind-hearted and willing to help others.

9. Never let your standards drop. By acting like the best, you're more likely to become one of the best.

10. Always be willing to help out. Ask your coach if they need a spare pair of hands with anything, such as pumping up the balls or collecting in the cones at the end of a session.

At your next training session or match, see how many of these tips you can tick off. Give yourself a big pat on the back (or a special Son handshake) if you get full marks!

Being brilliant at football is impressive, but as the former England women's manager and Manchester United legend Phil Neville says, "being a good person is the most important thing".

In a sport where so much comes down to luck, the way you dress and behave could be the difference between a scout taking a chance on you or passing you by.

Are you willing to take the risk?

# STORY OF A SUPERSTAR

# MEGAN RAPINOE

## THE ULTIMATE LIVING WELL PRO

**W**ow, talk about feeding your brain, eh? What a feast of delicious football information! In this section, you've learned about lots of different ways to live smart like your heroes. But before you nod off and get a good night's sleep like Agüero, here's a bedtime story about a true and fearless American icon, both on and off the football (or should we say, soccer?) pitch. Alongside winning two World Cups and an Olympic Gold Medal, **Megan Rapinoe** has also used her platform to speak out for social justice and equality for all.

Megan grew up in California playing soccer with her brother Brian and twin sister Rachael, but it was only years later at the University of Portland that she discovered her second great passion: politics. And the more she learned about the different kinds of discrimination and injustice in the world, the more she felt the need to do something about it. She wanted to stand up and speak out, but would it harm her future football career? No. Megan decided that she could do both: become a soccer star *and* a powerful political activist.

But in order to do both to the best of her ability, "Pinoe", as she's known, needed to live smart and get professional. At university, she was way too busy mixing sport and politics to do much late-night partying. Even on her twenty-first birthday, she said no to any wild celebrations. Why?

Because Megan was only two weeks away from making her senior debut for the USA and she wanted to focus on her training instead. That's dedication right there.

She did still find the time to feed her brain, though. Megan kept educating herself about important issues like racism, sexism, pay discrimination, the criminal justice system and the environment. She continued her quest for knowledge even when her sporting career took off and filled most of her time; and even when she had to fight her way back to full fitness after each of her three serious knee injuries. Megan's interest in politics didn't distract her from her football dream; in fact, it spurred her on. Because she knew that the more successful and famous she became as a sports star, the more impact her words would have when she spoke out on important issues. Or as Pinoe herself puts it: "The better you play, the more you win, and the bigger your platform becomes." So, after the video of her brilliant, last-minute assist for **Abby Wambach** in the 2011 World Cup match against Brazil went viral, Megan used her fame to come out as the first openly gay player on the US Women's National Team. "It's about standing up and being counted and saying you're proud of who you are," she said.

Four years later, after helping the USA to win the 2015 World Cup on her thirtieth birthday, Megan decided that the time was right to stand up and fight for equal pay. The

USA were the World Champions, so why were they earning so little money compared to the country's less successful men's team?

Then, on 5 September 2016, Megan made an even braver move by becoming the first non-Black sportsperson to take a knee during the American national anthem. It was a symbol of support for the American football star **Colin Kaepernick** and his protest against racial injustice in the USA. She too believed in equality for everyone, no matter what race, religion, gender or sexuality.

At first, it looked like that courageous act might have ended Megan's international football career. She was dropped from the USA squad and suddenly her dream of playing in a third World Cup was in doubt. But Megan didn't give up or stop speaking out; no, she just worked harder than ever on her football fitness. She began training with her girlfriend, basketball star **Sue Bird**, and eating exactly what she ate – more vegetables and less sugar and other carbohydrates. Megan found that her new healthy diet gave her so much more energy and the results were remarkable: "One look at me and it was blatantly obvious: I was stronger and leaner than before."

Soon, she was playing so well for her club, Seattle Reign, that her country just couldn't say no to her any more. With their star winger and strong leader back, Team USA didn't lose a single game in 2018. Megan grabbed nineteen goals and assists along the way. Yes, she was hitting top form just in time for the 2019 World Cup!

As the tournament approached, the USA women's national team continued their battle for equal pay. Although it was turning out to be a long and frustrating fight, the experience had actually brought the players closer together, creating a team bond that was stronger than ever. They weren't going to let politics distract them or divide them. No, they were fully focused on football, and determined to win the World Cup again.

Megan and her team-mates showed it by starting the tournament in style. At the final whistle in their first match, the scoreboard read: USA 13–0 Thailand. Wow, they had set a new World Cup scoring record! While Alex Morgan grabbed the headlines with five goals in the game, Megan bagged a hat-trick of assists, as well as a great goal of her own. After watching her shot hit the back of the net, she raced over to the bench to celebrate with all the USA substitutes, because winning was one big team effort.

And together, the USA team kept on winning:

**3–0 v. Chile …**      **2–0 v. Sweden …**      **2–1 v. Spain.**

They were through to yet another World Cup quarter-final, this time against the tournament hosts, France. It was already a massive match for the USA, but it became even bigger when a video was released where Megan said that she would refuse to visit the White House if they won the World Cup, in protest against the way the government treated women and Black people. That didn't go down well with the American president, Donald Trump, who replied angrily on Twitter, "Megan should WIN first before she TALKS! Finish the job!"

So, that's what she did, showing that not only can sport and politics mix, but they can sit side by side.

**GOAL!** She curled a clever free kick through the crowded penalty area and into the net.

With her dyed-pink hair dazzling and her arms outstretched, Megan stood in front of the fans, enjoying her moment in the spotlight. And there were more of those to come…

**GOAL!** She snuck in at the back post to calmly slot the ball past the French keeper.

Pinoe had done it. With the pressure on, she had led her team to victory! Now, they were just two games away from glory. Although she missed USA's semi-final win over

England, Megan returned for the biggest game of all: the final, against **Miedema**'s Netherlands team.

The score was still 0–0 at half-time, but Team USA stayed strong, united and full of belief. They knew they could do it; eventually, their golden chance would come.

In the sixtieth minute, **Morgan** was fouled as she challenged for the ball in the box – PENALTY! There was no doubt who would take it: their fearless leader with the powerful strike and the powerful voice.

Megan took a deep breath as she waited for the whistle. This was it, the chance they'd been waiting for. She wasn't just doing this for herself, for her team and for her country; she was doing it for everyone, for equality, respect and the right to be yourself. After a short run-up, she slotted her shot past the keeper. 1–0!

Once again, Megan stood in front of the fans, stretched her arms out and smiled. Scoring the crucial goal in the World Cup final with over one billion people watching – what a wild way to celebrate her thirty-fourth birthday!

And after the final whistle, the gifts kept coming: the Golden Boot (awarded to the player with the highest number of goals), the Golden Ball (awarded to the best player) and, to top it all, a second World Cup winner's medal. It had taken so much courage, teamwork, dedication and drive to get there, but Megan was now one of the best, most famous and most inspiring footballers on the planet. And with the world paying attention, she once again took the opportunity to use her platform to spread her powerful message of peace: "We have to love more, hate less, listen more, talk less."

And that is some fantastic advice from a footballer who has made it her mission to live smart.

# SO ARE YOU READY TO LIVE SMART?

With premium fuel, your brain and body will be ready to give their best for longer, which could make all the difference between an agonizing defeat and a heroic victory.

But that's not to say you always have to stick to the advice in this section. Sometimes it's nice to eat a load of junk food or enjoy a really late sleepover with your friends. That's fine, so long as you're sensible with when, and how often, you treat yourself.

Living like a pro comes down to what you believe is most important in your life. For many professional footballers, football is and always was the most important thing in their lives. This meant that they made important decisions by asking the question: "Will doing this help me to become better at football?"

Along the way you may need to make tough decisions. A sleepover the night before a big game won't help you become better at football, but leaving the sleepover at 9 p.m. might be fine. Having a banana after dinner rather than a bar of chocolate won't instantly transform you into Fran Kirby, but it's a habit that might help you get closer to her level.

Over time these small changes can make big differences.

## TOP TEN TIPS FOR LIVING SMART:

1. Enjoy a balanced diet that includes at least five portions of fruit and veg a day.

2. Drink lots of water each day to stay hydrated.

3. Make time to switch off from football and learn new skills.

4. Spend time with your friends and family.

5. Hang out with your team-mates when you're not at football together.

6. Read books and learn from the stories.

7. Give your body plenty of time to rest and recover between matches and training sessions.

8. Use the magical powers of sleep, making sure you get at least the recommended daily amount for your age.

9. Show respect to everyone — from your team-mates to the referee.

10. Stay positive and encourage the people around you.

## ULTIMATE CHALLENGES TO LIVE SMART:

1.  Give yourself a go in the kitchen! Learn to make one meal full of carbohydrates and protein, then test how soon before a game you should eat it to give you the most energy (around three hours before kick-off is a good starting point, but everyone's different).

2.  Read a book, listen to a podcast or watch a documentary about one of your favourite players each month and learn how they achieved their goals. What can you take from their journey?

3.  Discover a non-football activity that you and at least one of your support network can enjoy together.

4.  At your next game, shake the hand of the coach to say "hello" and ask if there's anything you can help with. Perhaps you can bring some of the equipment out to the pitch or help to lay out the kit?

5.  Go to sleep at the same time each night and set your alarm for the same time each morning – even at the weekends!

# MAKE EVERY GAME A TEN OUT OF TEN

Here, finally, comes the moment you've been waiting and preparing for. You've spent hours honing your game in practice sessions. You've trained your mind so it's at the top of its game. You've looked after your body so that it's ready to give everything. Now it's time to play smart.

You're lined up in your usual position on the pitch, ready for the game to start. You can still taste the banana/snack that you just shovelled down to give you some last-minute energy. Nerves are running through your body, but you know how to turn all that anxiety into excitement. You can't wait to put into practice everything that you've learned.

The whistle blows, the match kicks off.

Crunch time.

Everything comes down to these ninety minutes.

In just the same way that everything comes down to this chapter.

So let's become a hero and embrace the challenge!

Who do you see across the other side of the pitch? Are they bigger than you? Have you heard that they're better? Well, fear not! We're about to tell you how to outwit your opponents. Because they may just live up to the famous words of legendary manager Brian Clough: "... a good team on paper. Unfortunately, the game was played on grass."

That's the beauty of football – anyone can win. And by sticking to their strengths and making the most of their opponents' weaknesses, anyone can play well.

So, you want to go from "good" to "brilliant" in only a few pages? We're here to help!

In this section, we'll talk you through four important areas of performance. Really, there are hundreds of different areas we could have chosen. Seth believes that these are the four that have helped him the most, though:

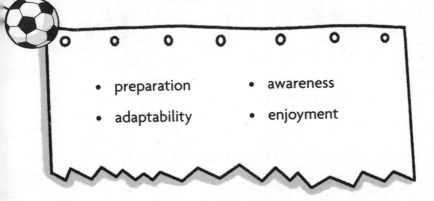

- preparation
- adaptability
- awareness
- enjoyment

Can you capture the magic you show in training and transfer it to the pitch when it matters most?

Believe you can and you're halfway there...

# 01 PLAY LIKE KANTÉ
## MASTER THE 5 "P"s

## N'GOLO KANTÉ

**NATIONALITY:** French

**POSITION:** Defensive Midfielder

**HERO MOMENT:** stopping opponents in their tracks, helping France to win the 2018 World Cup

For footballers, it's really important to learn to "P"... No, not like that! We're on about the "P" that stands for **prepare**. What on earth were you thinking of?! A match doesn't only start when the referee blows their whistle. Preparations start long before that. You've already been preparing as you read this book, for example. And to do the job well, there are, in fact, five "P"s to consider: **p**roper **p**reparation **p**revents **p**oor **p**erformance.

Pep Guardiola, one of the greatest managers in the game, said, "If you train badly, you play badly. If you work like a beast in training, you play the same way." When you've prepared as well as you can, you're able to play without any worries. You don't yawn your way through the warm-up; you don't suffer from self-doubt. Instead, you work as hard as you can, giving your all to help your team win.

Sounds simple, right? But what can you do to make sure you're ready to perform at your best? Well, let's take a closer look at the pre-match preparations of France's World Cup winner **N'Golo Kanté**, one of the hardest-working footballers in the world. As a defensive midfielder, his job is to run, and run, and run, making lots of amazing tackles and interceptions to stop the other team from attacking. When it comes to winning the ball back, Kanté is one of the best in the business, but he doesn't just walk onto the pitch and magically play well.

No, top footballers prepare for days, sometimes even weeks, leading up to a match. Kanté knows that he has to train smart, think smart and live smart in order to play smart. As we've already learned in this book, that means:

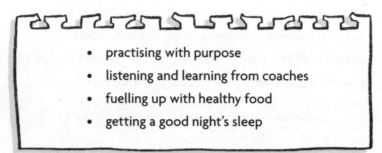

- practising with purpose
- listening and learning from coaches
- fuelling up with healthy food
- getting a good night's sleep

But that's just for starters; a player's preparation then ramps up even further for the main event – match day.

# Football Fairy Tale:
## The Player Who Failed to Prepare

Once upon a time, a defender called **Phil Neville** woke up to his worst nightmare. He discovered that he was going to be on the bench for Manchester United's Champions League qualifier! That made him angry. What was the point in preparing properly if he was going to be a sub? Instead of taking a nap before the game as usual, he spoke to friends on the phone. He ate more food than he normally would. He didn't even wear his lucky pants.

Just a few minutes into the match, **Wes Brown** injured himself and suddenly Phil was subbed onto the pitch. He tried to play his usual game, but without his proper preparation he performed poorly. With the clock ticking and the game still at 0–0, Phil made a mistake that cost his team dearly. They lost the match 1–0.

Phil's story shows how important it is to prepare properly. He had the wrong mindset, the wrong sleep, the wrong diet.

If he'd stuck to his usual routine Manchester United might have drawn 0–0. If he'd listened to the pre-match team talk so he understood the players' positions, they may even have won. And if only he had worn his lucky pants, then who knows?! THE END.

# CHOOSE YOUR STRATEGY

Right, listen up, everyone – it's time for the pre-match team talk! That's where the whole team comes together to talk about how they are going to win the match. The manager might start by going over previous performances – what the players did well, and what they could do better. They'll probably also say lots of motivational things like "Come on!" and "We can beat these bozos!" but the main focus will be on the tactics for the latest match, the strategy for success.

As Kanté explains, a key part of preparing for a match is thinking about "all the tactical aspects we need to repeat. Our concentration on game day is basically remembering what we've been working on."

That's right, the pros in the Premier League spend lots of time in training practising the best ways to win. Each opponent will have a different style, and different strengths and weaknesses, so teams change the way that they play – and prepare – accordingly. Maybe the manager has a crazy idea to try a new formation with seven midfielders, or perhaps they want their team to sit deep so that they can counter-attack.

With tactics changing all the time, it means that individual players must be able to constantly adapt. When you play against a team that is better than you and BIGGER than you, then it is even more important to plan how you are going to win as a team. Against better players, it's important to be confident. Play to your strengths, try your hardest to hide any weaknesses and look for their weaknesses instead.

The same goes for bigger opponents. A tall player might be better at winning headers, for example, but they might not be so good at winning sprint races. At 1.68 metres (5 feet 6 inches), Kanté is one of the smallest players in the Premier

League. As a youngster in France, he was told that he was too small to ever become a top footballer. But now, ten years later, he's a two-time Premier League champion and a World Cup winner who regularly wins his battles against massive midfielders like Rodri and Paul Pogba (both 1.91 metres or 6 feet 3 inches).

So how does he do it? By preparing so he's ready for the challenge. Kanté knows that he's not going to win many headers against the big boys, but that's not his style anyway. Instead, he plays to his strengths:

**Speed –** Kanté might not be able to outjump many midfielders but he can certainly outrun most of them. He's one of the fastest players in the Premier League, especially when there's an attacker to be chased and a ball to be won back (most managers like their players to win the ball back within six seconds of losing it. This prevents the opponents from getting organized in an attack and makes you more likely to win the ball further up the field!).

**Energy** – Not only can Kanté run fast, but he can keep running fast for the whole game. Not many midfielders can match his stamina or his work rate. When Kanté first arrived at Leicester City, his manager **Claudio Ranieri** couldn't believe it – "he was running so hard that I thought he must have a pack full of batteries hidden in his shorts!" When Kanté signed for Chelsea, **Eden Hazard** joked, "I think sometimes when I'm on the pitch I see him twice. One on the left, one on the right. I think I'm playing with twins!" That's one of his team-mates talking; imagine how his opponents must feel!

**Intelligence** – Being quick and energetic is great, but you need to understand football too if you want to win the midfield battle. Luckily, Kanté reads the game really well and so he knows what's going to happen before it even happens. This means he gets himself into the right positions to steal the ball. He's so small, clever and speedy that often he can sneak in before his opponent has even seen him!

# GAME-TIME

So, how can you learn to play to your strengths like Kanté and hide your weaknesses? We've come up with a few ideas to help you prepare for your next match.

| Strengths | Strategy |
|---|---|
| If you are quick... | Make the pitch wide and sprint into the space that your opponents leave (especially if their defence is high up the pitch). |
| If you have a great first touch... | Take the ball in tight spaces. This will draw in your opponents and create space elsewhere. |
| If you have a powerful shot... | Use it! Accurate shots from outside the area scare an opponent and make them change the way they defend. |
| If you are bigger than your opponents... | Get the ball out wide for crosses into the box. |
| If you can dribble well... | Choose the opponents' weakest defender and get yourself into one-on-one situations with them. However, when you receive the ball, make your next decision wisely. It's not always a good idea to take on a defender; one of your team-mates might be in a better position than you! |
| If you have energy to burn... | Don't allow your opponents a second to think. Press them cleverly. |

| Weaknesses | Strategy |
|---|---|
| If you aren't the quickest... | Get close to your opponent when they have the ball and don't allow them any space. |
| If you are smaller than your opponents... | Keep the ball on the floor and play short, sharp passes to drag your opponents in and create space for a through ball. In defence, press your opponents high up the pitch so they have less time to pick out a pass. |
| If you are lacking energy... | Sit back and conserve your energy, defending your half and chasing forward when needed (it's important the rest of your team also sits back). |
| If you aren't yet comfortable on the ball... | Start off by playing simple passes. As your confidence grows, you can try riskier balls. |
| If you rarely win the ball when defending... | Stay on your feet. Delay your opponent until one of your defenders provides cover. Show them to whichever side you feel is least dangerous. |

You'll notice that all of these tips involve your team-mates. When you work as a team, you can't do anything alone – you have to do it together.

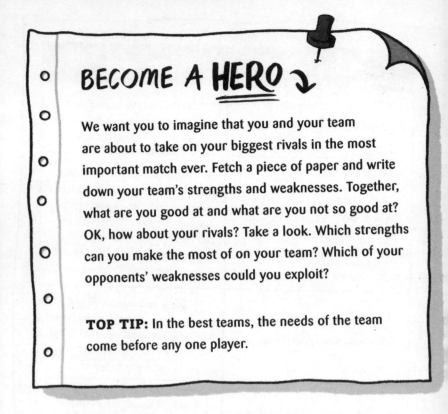

# BECOME A HERO ⤵

We want you to imagine that you and your team are about to take on your biggest rivals in the most important match ever. Fetch a piece of paper and write down your team's strengths and weaknesses. Together, what are you good at and what are you not so good at? OK, how about your rivals? Take a look. Which strengths can you make the most of on your team? Which of your opponents' weaknesses could you exploit?

**TOP TIP:** In the best teams, the needs of the team come before any one player.

If everything goes to plan, teamwork will make the DREAM WORK. Even against the toughest of opponents!

These plans are all discussed before a match even kicks off. They make up part of the five "P"s. In all of the plans, it's vitally important that all of the team work together. Every single person plays a part in attacking and defending, as well as in highlighting strengths and hiding weaknesses. Even the substitutes, whose job is to stay alert in case they come onto the pitch, watch what the opponents are doing, as well as shouting encouragement from the side and celebrating the team's successes. As Wales midfielder **Aaron Ramsey** puts it, "When you prepare properly and give everything you've got, you feel strong going into any match. If every player feels like that then the team will have a collective strength and determination."

Of course, there are always going to be uncontrollables. Opponents may have unexpected tactics or a new, amazing player in their team. That's why it's important to prepare multiple plans for different situations. And, as we're about to find out, it's why it's so important to be adaptable.

# 02 PLAY LIKE BRONZE
## ENJOY EVERY POSITION ON THE PITCH

## LUCY BRONZE

**NATIONALITY:** English

**POSITION:** Defender

**HERO MOMENT:** winning the Treble with Lyon *and* the Best FIFA Women's Player award in 2020!

Attackers attack and defenders defend, right? Wrong!

Well, maybe way back when footballs were made of pig's bladders (this actually happened!). But not now. In the modern game, players have to be able to adapt to any position on the pitch! Full-backs mark wingers then race forward to whip in crosses. Centre-backs stop dangerous attacks then play clever through balls to strikers. Wingers dazzle with trickery but also track back to help out the defence. Central midfielders run from box to box, shooting at goal but also making interceptions.

These days, every player is expected to both attack and defend. Even goalkeepers!

Once again, it all comes down to teamwork. It's easier to attack if you attack with all eleven players. That's why goalkeepers must now be comfortable with the ball at their feet. They need to take the ball under pressure and find passes, starting off attacks in their own half.

The same goes for defending. The next time you're watching Liverpool play and their opponents have the ball in their own half, keep a close eye on strikers **Mo Salah**, **Sadio Mané** and **Roberto Firmino**. Watch how hard they work to win it back. That's because if they're successful, they're closer to the opposition goal and therefore much more likely to shoot and score. A team's strikers actually make up their first line of defence. The midfielders are the next line, followed by the actual defence and then the goalkeeper, who has to be ready to rush out and deal with any danger.

It's important that players are comfortable in lots of different positions.

If you want a perfect example of this, look no further than England international, **Lucy Bronze**. She's really not your average right-back. She's so multi-talented that she used to make pizzas at Domino's while also studying at university *and* playing for Everton! But seriously, what makes the 2020 Best FIFA Women's Player such an all-round, adaptable footballer? Well, it's partly that she's played pretty much every position on the pitch.

When she first joined the Sunderland academy, aged eleven, Bronze was one of the fastest and fittest players in the squad and so the coaches asked her to play in attack. She did a decent job up front but there was one problem: scoring goals.

This might sound strange now if you saw her wonder-strike against Norway at the 2019 World Cup, but back then, Bronze was too shy to take the spotlight. Even if she was right in front of goal, she preferred to pass the ball to a team-mate instead.

"Maybe you're not a goal-scorer," her coaches decided.

OK, so what was her perfect position? To work out the answer, Bronze pretty much tried them all! At first, she moved into midfield, but by the time she joined Women Super League Champions Liverpool, aged twenty-one,

she had moved back even further and discovered her favourite role: defender. It was then that she realized something really important: "I enjoy stopping goals more than any of the goals I've scored."

Thanks to her fierce determination (fun fact: "Tough" is actually one of her middle names!) and brilliant football brain, Bronze started out as **Steph Houghton**'s centre-back partner for England. But it soon became clear that the national team also needed her speed and skill further up the pitch. During the 2015 World Cup, she played on the wing. She recalls, "At the time **Alex Scott** had been England right-back for as long as I could remember, so I had to work out where I could fit in, as I'd rather be on the pitch than not at all." But

when Scott retired in 2017, Bronze made the right-back role her own.

The position was perfect for her. It allowed her to play to all her different strengths at the same time: running and tackling, but also dribbling and crossing. Now, not only is Bronze one of England's best defenders, but she's also one of their most dangerous attackers too. Starting from a deeper position on the pitch, she makes the most of that extra space to speed her way up the wing.

While right-back is her favourite role, Bronze is still willing and able to play anywhere on the pitch. In fact, she finds the challenge of adapting to new positions exciting. For England, she often moves forward into central midfield when the team needs her to take control of the game. What a useful hero to have!

Bronze also showed a different type of adaptability in 2017, when she decided to leave Manchester City and move to France to play for Olympique Lyonnais. She was determined to settle in straight away, so she set about learning the language and absorbing the local culture, as well as enjoying the warm weather. It worked, because Bronze helped her team to win three UEFA Women's Champions League titles in a row! Now, she's back at Manchester City and looking to win even more trophies.

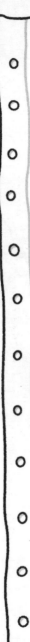

# BECOME A HERO ↲

- If your favourite position is as a striker, then have a go at playing in defence. By marking an opposing striker, you'll find out which runs are easy to defend against and which movements are more challenging. When you then go back to playing as a striker, you'll be able to try out the movements that you found so hard to defend against. You'll also be better at defending from the front and might win the ball back in really dangerous positions.

- If you usually play on the left of the pitch, have a go on the right, and vice versa. The different side will help you improve your weak foot, as well as learn to attack and defend by showing opponents onto your left and right sides.

- If you're usually a defender, have a go in midfield. When you play in midfield, the game goes on all around you. There are constantly opponents running around while the ball moves back and forth. This means there are loads of 1 v. 1 and 2 v. 2 situations. Interceptions and tackles are vital. Yet in defence, the game almost always happens in front of you. Trying out in midfield helps you to "play 360".

# DO IT ALL!

You never know, you may end up being better in a different position, just as Bronze and these other football heroes discovered:

- Spanish goalkeeper **David de Gea** grew up playing as a striker as well as between the sticks. That's probably why he's so good at saving shots with his feet!
- England right-back **Trent Alexander-Arnold** often played in central midfield during his Liverpool youth team days, which helped develop his creativity and turned him into an assist king when he moved back into defence.
- Manchester United and England right-back **Aaron Wan-Bissaka** used to be a winger, which helped him to become an amazing full-back.
- England captain **Steph Houghton** started out as a striker, before moving into midfield and then all the way back into defence.
- Welsh superstar **Gareth Bale** was a handy left-back who became the world's most expensive player after transforming into a left-winger.
- Arsenal legend **Thierry Henry** was a good winger, then became a phenomenal striker. The same goes for **Cristiano Ronaldo**.

Sometimes, as in Bronze's case, your coach might spot your potential to play better in a different position. But sometimes, you may have to be brave and ask to try something new. Remember, when you're starting out, it is most important that you improve in games, rather than win them. You probably won't remember winning 2–0 against that other Under-13s team, but you will remember what you learned from playing in a new position.

The Dutch club Ajax, which has what is considered one of the best youth academies in the world, understands the importance of playing lots of different positions. Their youth players play in a triangle of three roles in one season. They may start off at right-back, then move to centre-back before having a go on the wing. Their players gain a fuller understanding of the game as a result.

## STAY OUT OF THE BOX

Some players automatically get put in positions because of how they look. A big player is more likely to be put in defence, while a fast player is most likely to be put on the wing. Players are told they're too small to play in goal or not tall enough to play at centre-back. We call this being put into a box. You should never let this happen to you.

First of all, players have growth spurts at different times. Someone smaller than average can suddenly become the tallest player in their team over a summer. The biggest player in a youth team probably won't end up being the biggest player in their adult team.

Second, football is constantly changing. Previously, it was believed that centre-backs have to be super tall so they can head clearances away. Now, coaches like Pep Guardiola play small players at centre-back (and in goal!).

Wherever you end up playing in a game, it's vital to understand your role and responsibility. You can ask your coach what they'd like to see you trying. Watching professional players and paying attention to what they do when playing that position can also help you.

And if you learn a new position really well, it can help you get lots of game-time in the future. It also means that you can help out the team by covering for players who are injured. Basically, if you can become as adaptable as Bronze, then you'll spend much less time on the bench!

At first, it'll be hard. Everything will feel weird, and even the pitch will look different. You may find you're not as good in the new position, or you don't enjoy it as much. But, just like our heroes, you'll end up being a far better footballer.

# 03 PLAY LIKE XAVI

## ALWAYS BE AWARE

## XAVI

**NATIONALITY:** Spanish

**POSITION:** Midfielder

**HERO MOMENT:** playing 599 accurate passes in seven matches as Spain won the 2010 World Cup

Have you ever felt like your teachers have eyes in the back of their heads? We certainly have. Whenever we felt like mucking around a bit at the back of the class (we were good boys, really!), somehow they still knew exactly what we were doing – even though they were facing the opposite direction!

How did they do that?

Because of their awareness.

That's something that they share with the world's best footballers. Awareness is knowing what's around you at all times, which helps you to anticipate what is about to happen. Once you anticipate it, you can then snap into action once it does happen (or even better, just before it's about to happen!).

**awareness**          **anticipation**          **action**

How about right now? Do you know what's happening all around you? If you're the only person in the room, then that's easy. Now we want you to test yourself.

# BECOME A HERO ↓

Take this book into a room where there are other people. We want you to try and read it while staying aware of what the other people in the room are doing. It's kind of hard, right? You have to keep on looking up from these pages and checking left, right, in front and behind, like you're crossing a busy road. And the people all keep moving! If you really want to test yourself, try to note down what the people are wearing and the actions they are making – all while continuing to read the book. It might not seem related to football, but what you're actually doing is practising for when you get onto the pitch.

That's because on a pitch there are twenty-one players all around you. Plus a ball. And a referee. Ten of them are on your team. Eleven aren't. Just like the people in the room you're in, everyone keeps moving around. And to make things even harder, so does the ball.

## SEE THE PICTURES

Knowing where as many of the players are at any one time, plus the ball, helps you to anticipate what is about to happen. To do this, the world's best players scan the pitch. They check over their shoulders, then behind them, so they can create pictures in their heads of what's going on in the match. As players move, the picture changes, meaning they need to make new runs to receive the ball or move to new spaces to stop dangerous attacks. They keep on scanning throughout the whole game.

How many times do you think they scan in a ninety-minute match?

Go on, have a guess.

We bet you won't be anywhere near.

Because the correct answer is so high that we almost fell off our chairs. (If only we'd had the awareness to anticipate such a big number, hahaha!)

804.

That's right. In a game against Real Zaragoza, former Barcelona midfield maestro **Xavier Hernández Creus**, better known as "**Xavi**", scanned his surroundings 804 times. That's nine times every minute. Once every 6.71641816 seconds. Which is about how long it took you to read this sentence.

Scanning so much meant that Xavi often knew exactly what was going to happen. When he received the ball, he made everything look so easy. He always seemed to make the right decision. He never seemed rushed. And it's all thanks to scanning. "Think quickly, look for spaces. That's what I do: look for space. All day."

Xavi was only eleven years old when he joined the Barcelona academy and started learning to play the **Johan Cruyff** way. Cruyff, a legend for the Dutch national

team as well as for his club, Barcelona, later became the manager of the Catalan giants. He designed their youth system, following the belief that "football is a game you play with your mind". That suited Xavi perfectly. He was never going to be the tallest or the strongest or the fastest player in the team, so he set out to be the cleverest instead.

Lots and lots of hard work and rondos later (we talked about those in Train Smart, remember?), Xavi was ready to join the Barcelona first team. Early in his career, people said he wasn't good enough to replace **Pep Guardiola** in midfield, but he kept going until they changed their minds. Then along came another talented young passmaster, Andrés Iniesta. Uh-oh, was there really room for both of them at Barcelona?

Yes! Together they went on to win seven league titles and four Champions League trophies for their club, as well as a World Cup and two Euros for their country, Spain.

Iniesta was the more attacking of the two midfielders, known for his dribbling and movement. And Xavi? "My greatest quality is my mental speed." Like all top midfielders, he anticipated exactly what he was going to do before he even received the ball. Because he looked around so much, Xavi always had two or three options in his mind. All this information allowed him to think quickly and make a good decision when the ball arrived. It's no coincidence that the world's best players are also the world's quickest thinkers.

**TOP TIP:** The better your awareness of your surroundings, the more likely you are to make a good decision. Get a 360-degree view of what's around you to be at your most effective.

# READ THE GAME

Any decision that Xavi made was based on the picture in his head from his most recent scan of the pitch. If he knew that an opponent was close to him, then he'd shield the ball and quickly play it off to a team-mate with one or two touches. If there was space behind him, however, he'd open his body to turn. He was also fully aware of what his team-mates were going to do. If he'd seen out of the corner of his eye that Messi was making a forward run, for example, he could play a first-time pass without looking up. He'd know which of his team-mates were in space, which ones wanted the ball, where they were going to run to, if they would stay onside and whether they wanted the ball passed to their feet or forward into space.

Before receiving the ball, he'd check over his shoulder one final time, then take action. By making a decision so quickly, it was really hard for defenders to get organized and stop what he was going to do.

# QUIZ TIME

### Which player is playing smarter?

**Player A:** Has eyes only for the ball. Stands and admires passes. Decides what to do only after receiving the ball. Reacts to danger after it has happened. Always faces play.

**Player B:** Passes and moves into new space. Checks over their shoulders every few seconds. Already knows what they're doing before receiving the ball. Checks over their shoulders again. Anticipates danger. Opens their body up to see as much of the pitch as possible.

The answer is Player B. Top players like Player B don't stand still and admire their work. They constantly buzz about the pitch, always looking for space to play in and forward passes to make.

Players like Player A are much easier to defend against. That's because when they do get the ball, they then have to look up then process what's going on in the game. At the top level, everything happens so fast that by the time they've delayed their decision, their opponents have had time to get organized and are all over them like a really horrible rash.

They're also much easier to attack against. Without checking over their shoulders, they don't know what kinds of runs the attackers are making. This makes it easier for forwards to fool them and create lots of space to run into.

So always check over your shoulders when defending, as well as attacking. This keeps you alert to danger and also helps you anticipate what is about to happen. Opponents always give you clues. By looking at a player's body language, for instance, you can tell where they're about to kick the ball. (Usually, their hips are pointing in the direction they'll play the pass.)

The good news? You too can improve your scanning and awareness so that you always know what is happening on the pitch.

## BECOME A HERO ↲

Next time you're at training, try checking your shoulders every few seconds to know what is going on around you. It doesn't matter which position you're playing in. Get into the habit of looking behind you before receiving a pass so that you know whether to shield the ball from an opponent or to turn into the space. Soon enough, your team-mates will know that they can pass it to you and that you'll make the right decision.

# 04 PLAY LIKE VAN DIJK
## KEEP CALM AND HAVE FUN

# VIRGIL VAN DIJK

**NATIONALITY:** Dutch

**POSITION:** Defender

**HERO MOMENT:** keeping twenty-one clean sheets in his first season on Liverpool's defence

Football is fun. That's why you started to play the game in the first place. And as we said earlier in the Think Smart section, you'll play your best when you relax and enjoy being on the pitch.

By "enjoy" and "fun", we don't mean telling jokes to the referee or your team-mates. Even if they're really good ones.

Which football team loves ice cream? *Aston Vanilla!*

What do footballers love to drink? *Penal-tea!*

What's a goalkeeper's favourite snack? *Beans on post!*

OK, that was pretty fun. But not as fun as playing without any worries and with the full confidence to express yourself. Just like **Virgil van Dijk**.

He's a cool, calm leader, both for his club, Liverpool, and his country, the Netherlands. Van Dijk is a tall, quick and very clever defender. He doesn't let anything faze him; not even playing in massive Champions League matches against Messi and Ronaldo. How? His method is simple: "keep working hard, stay humble. I think in games you need to turn nervous feelings to more excitement anyway, otherwise you're going to limit your ability to play.

You're going to put it in your head that you don't want to make mistakes and normally then you're going to make mistakes."

So, let go of your worries and listen to Van Dijk's words of football wisdom: "The most important thing is to enjoy it. We have to give it our all and make sure we have no regrets at the end of it."

When the pressure is really on in the Premier League, he often thinks back to his childhood and the good times he had playing endless games with his friends in his hometown, Breda. It's his way of reminding himself what football is all about – fun!

When you believe in yourself like Van Dijk, you don't let anything affect the way you play your game. Match day is no different from all the training sessions and fun kick-abouts you've had with your mates. Your control is the same, your dribbling is the same, your blocks are the same. The movements are movements that have been repeated millions of times. They come naturally now.

**TOP TIP:** Focusing on what you do well means playing your own game. If you try to play someone else's game, they'll probably be better at it than you!

# BELIEVE IN YOURSELF

These days, Van Dijk is known as one of the most dependable defenders in the world, but once upon a time, his calm confidence was seen as a problem. As a youngster, his coaches at Willem II and Groningen often told him to try harder and concentrate on the game. But Van Dijk knew that he wasn't too laid-back or lazy; it just looked that way because he did a little less running and a lot more watching.

Inside his head, Van Dijk is 100% concentrated on the game. He's alert to every danger and is constantly making predictions about what will happen. One of the things that makes him such a confident defender is that he looks for triggers.

A trigger is a sign of weakness in your opponent. Maybe they're taking lots of touches, which shows they're unsure what to do. Perhaps the ball is on their weak foot and they don't look comfortable. They could be running into a defensive overload.

Van Dijk can even cause these

triggers. By moving his body in certain ways, he can force an opponent to run in a direction he chooses by blocking off one side of the pitch. When he's defending in the opponents' half, he'll usually get arms-length from his opponent and block off the path down the line. This forces them into the middle of the pitch, where he knows that there are loads of team-mates who can help him win the ball. When he's defending near his own goal, he'll usually block off the middle of the pitch and stay goal-side (between the ball and the goal). This will keep the opponent away from a dangerous position where they can shoot at goal and force them instead to stay out wide. Clever, right? And as a defender, what's more fun than winning your battle against a striker and stealing the ball?

# BECOME A HERO ↵

You don't need an opponent to practise your ultimate Van Dijk defensive body shape. All you need is a ball.

- Start from a distance of 10 metres away. Sprint to the ball, slowing down and taking lots of small steps when you get closer. This helps you to change direction more easily. The quicker you get there, the less time an opponent will have to think.

- When you're within touching distance of the ball, reach out with your arm and move your body position so that you are sideways. Either your right foot will be to the right of the ball or your left foot will be to the left of the ball, with the other directly behind. Practise both ways. Sometimes you'll need to block off your opponent's right side so they have to move left; other times you'll need to block off their left side.

- Your body shape should be such that an opponent would be forced in one direction.

- Once you're happy with constant training, progress to varied training where you're playing against a single opponent. Work on getting within touching distance and moving your body shape to force them in a certain direction. Can you spot a trigger to steal the ball, such as when they dribble onto their weaker foot?

When Van Dijk spots a trigger, he knows that he can pounce to win the ball. This also helps him to stay calm. He knows that the right moment will come, so long as he stays patient and doesn't dive in. He just has to focus on what happens in front of him and force his opponent into making a mistake.

## KEEP CALM

When Van Dijk is defending, there's no room in his head for doubt. By keeping himself so calm, he can think clearly and cleverly about what he needs to do next, and then take confident action. No, he doesn't always make the right decision, but simply making a decision allows the rest of the team to react. It's better to make a bad decision than to make no decision at all.

Even the best players sometimes make bad decisions. Van Dijk has misjudged back passes that have resulted in his team conceding goals, he has given away penalty kicks and missed important tackles. But top defenders don't dwell on their errors; they shrug them off and go again.

And the same is true with awesome attackers like Tottenham and England's **Dele Alli.** He demands the ball because he's confident that he can make the difference for his team. Alli doesn't mind if there are opponents pressuring him because that's all part of the challenge: "You can't go out onto the pitch and hide. You need to get on the ball and enjoy it... I believe in my ability. So when things aren't going my way, I just keep going, keep asking for the ball and keep trying things."

Even if Alli makes a few mistakes in a row, he still demands the ball. Rather than trying a defence-splitting pass, though, he might play an easy five-yard pass to build his confidence back up again. But soon enough, he's back taking risks.

## CREATE CONFIDENCE IN OTHERS

No matter what happens in the game, Virgil always plays with a smile on his face. That's because when you play with a smile on your face, you're more likely to play with confidence. And confidence is infectious; it can quickly rub off on the rest of your team. Ever since Van Dijk arrived at Anfield in January 2018 for £75 million, his calm presence has helped make the Liverpool backline rock solid. Not only does he get the best out of himself in the big games, but he also gets the best out of the young defenders alongside him, especially his centre-back partner, **Joe Gomez**, who said: "... it's a massive help and a confidence booster just having someone like him beside you."

Some of Van Dijk's influence comes from his strong body language and calmness on the ball, but a lot of it also comes from his communication. If you watch him play, he never shuts up! He's always talking to his team-mates, giving them encouragement and advice, like:

Well done!

Why don't you try that turn again?

Have you thought about playing on the shoulder of the last defender?

Great effort!

Step up!

Keep going!

Watch out for that striker on your left shoulder!

Some of these examples are instructive. They provide players with information that helps them to make instant decisions. Some of the examples encourage team-mates. This keeps their motivation and enjoyment high and makes them more likely to give their all.

## BECOME A HERO ↴

Next time you're on the pitch, why don't you try and encourage your team-mates? If you tell them important instructions, such as where their opponents are, it makes it easier for them to play their game. Keep it simple and make sure you add value with what you say, rather than just commentating on the game.

When you enjoy yourself on the pitch like Virgil, you can produce beautiful moments. Think England legend **David Beckham**'s goal from the halfway line, Swedish superstar Zlatan Ibrahimovic's overhead kick against England, or even Van Dijk's perfect 2 v. 1 defending against Tottenham's **Moussa Sissoko** and Son Heung-min. Beautiful moments, accompanied by beautiful smiles — because there's nothing more fun than playing a game of football in your own unique way.

# STORY OF A SUPERSTAR

# CRISTIANO RONALDO

## THE ULTIMATE HERO ON THE PITCH

N ow you know what it takes to play smart like your heroes – preparation, adaptability, belief and awareness. But we couldn't blabber on about performing at your best without telling you the story of one of the greatest players of them all, **Cristiano Ronaldo**.

We'll start way back in 2002, just as Cristiano was taking his first steps in the Sporting Lisbon first team as a skilful seventeen-year-old.

The manager, **László Bölöni**, liked Cristiano's speed and dribbling, but he knew that the youngster was going to need more than that to perform well in Portugal's Primeira Liga. So he wrote down a long list of things that Cristiano needed to improve, including: heading, defending, physical strength, mental strength, teamwork, tactics.

Instead of complaining, Cristiano set to work, never changing his unique style but challenging himself to become a better all-round player. The practice paid off. By the end of his first season at Sporting, he had scored five goals and set up three more for his team-mates.

That summer, the mighty Manchester United came to Lisbon. They were there to play a friendly against Sporting to open their new stadium, but that wasn't the only reason for the visit. Their manager **Sir Alex Ferguson** was also there to watch a new young winger.

At the age of only eighteen, Cristiano could easily have panicked and played badly in the big match against Manchester United. But no, he was too calm and confident to feel nervous. Instead, he was excited to go out there and prove himself. He slicked back his blond highlights, took one last look in the mirror, and told himself, "I'm ready!"

It was a night that Cristiano would never forget, and neither would United's right-back, **John O'Shea**, although for different reasons. With the spotlight on him, Sporting's Number 28 was able to hide his weaknesses – heading and defending – and play to his strengths – speed and skill.

"I need more help here!" O'Shea was soon shouting to his team-mates as Cristiano danced his way through the United defence again and again.

By the final whistle, the deal was done – he was a Manchester United star now!

However, Cristiano still had lots to learn, especially about playing in the Premier League. In England, he found that whenever he tried to do too many tricks, a defender would rush in and knock him off the ball.

"Just pass it!" the United strikers yelled angrily at him.

It was time for Cristiano to adapt his playing style again. He didn't have to cut out the skills entirely; no, he just had to focus on getting goals and assists first. That was how he would win games for his team and become a Manchester United hero.

From twelve goals during the 2005–06 season, he jumped to twenty-three the next year and then forty-two the year after that. Cristiano was a world-class superstar now!

Some of that improvement was due to a change of position. In his first few seasons at United, Ferguson had used him as a right-winger, but Cristiano preferred playing further forward in a front three. That formation gave him more freedom to move around the pitch, switching whenever he liked with **Wayne Rooney** and **Carlos Tevez**. Cristiano was now a defender's nightmare; he was so brilliant with both feet that he could shine on the left or right, or even through the middle as a striker.

But most of Cristiano's improvement was due to better preparation. He continued to work hard on those weaknesses that Bölöni had first noticed back in 2002. He spent hours in the gym building up his strength; he started chasing back more to help out his defenders, and he even scored a towering header as United won the 2008 Champions League final against Chelsea.

At the same time, Cristiano also got more tactical about the game he loved. He used visualization to improve the accuracy of his shooting and worked on his awareness of where his opponents were at all times. He also prepared for each match by picking out the weakest defenders to target.

In 2009, Cristiano decided it was time to move on from Manchester United after winning three Premier League titles. He signed for Real Madrid for £80 million, making him the most expensive player in the world at that time.

Some players might have felt the pressure, but not Cristiano. He knew that he was good enough to become a "Galáctico", the name given to Real Madrid's most expensive superstar signings. In Spain, against his greatest rival, Messi, he took his game to the next level. For six seasons in a row, Cristiano scored more than fifty goals! Cristiano was proving that he was one of the greatest big-game players, capable of scoring big-game goals, such as:

- the winner to beat Barcelona in the 2011 Copa del Rey final
- another winner against Barcelona to help Real Madrid lift the 2012 Spanish league title
- and then two goals in 2013 to knock his old club Manchester United out of the Champions League

Cristiano's self-belief soon spread throughout the Real Madrid squad. With CR7 in their team, the players felt confident that they could win any match, even in the biggest tournament of all: the Champions League. The club hadn't won the competition since 2002, but suddenly, they were unstoppable.

In 2014, Cristiano grabbed a goal and an assist as Real beat their local rivals, Atlético Madrid, in the 2014 Champions League final.

But in 2016, things weren't looking good when Real lost 2–0 to Wolfsburg in their quarter-final first leg. Back at the Bernabeu, Real's stadium, Cristiano turned things around

in the second leg by banging in yet another hat-trick! He then scored the winning penalty when the final went to a shoot-out – and they lifted the trophy again.

In 2017, Cristiano scored back-to-back hat-tricks against Bayern Munich and Atlético, before adding another two in the final against Juventus.

And in 2018, Real won the Champions League for a fourth time in five years. For once, Cristiano didn't score in the final, but again, his big-game goals had helped them get there.

One of the "secrets" of Cristiano's success is that he's never satisfied. He always wants to improve. As he got older (and wiser), he continued to adapt his style, becoming more of a classic centre-forward. He no longer had the super speed to dribble his way past defender after defender on the wing, but he was still brilliant at scoring goals.

So, Cristiano moved into the middle and worked hard on becoming a superstar striker instead. He practised his clever runs in between the centre-backs, he learned how to leap really high for headers (higher even than a lot of basketball players!) and he got really good at predicting what his team-mates and opposition would do next. So good, in fact, that Cristiano can score goals in the dark! In an experiment where the lights were turned off just as the ball was crossed in, he still managed to find the net, simply by looking at the winger's body shape. Amazing!

Even as he comes towards the end of his incredible career, Cristiano is still scoring lots of goals and finding new ways to improve, too. For example, when he was younger, Cristiano used to get really angry at his team-mates if they played the wrong pass or gave the ball away. That's because he expected everyone around him to be as brilliant as him. But these days, Cristiano is a better team player (well, most of the time, anyway!). He knows that, despite all his talent, he can't win football matches and tournaments on his own.

After leading Portugal all the way to the Euro 2016 final, Cristiano picked up an injury early in the match and left the field in tears. But no, that's not the end of the story. Instead of moping around in the dressing room, he spent the rest of the game leading his team-mates from the sidelines, offering them lots of encouragement and advice. When substitute striker **Ederzito Lopes**, or "**Eder**", was waiting to come on in extra time, Cristiano was busy building his team-mate's confidence by telling him, "You're going to score today." And what happened next? Yes, Eder grabbed the winning goal!

So, let Ronaldo be your football role model. You can still play smart even if you're not on the pitch.

# SO ARE YOU READY TO PLAY SMART?

Straight from kick-off, set the tempo. Give everything. Be hungry. Take a positive first touch. Smile. Enjoy! Anticipate.

It seems simple, doesn't it? That's because it is. Playing like your heroes isn't rocket science. They don't have any cheat codes tucked up their sleeves or superhuman abilities. They were once like you. Over the years they trained hard, thought smart, lived well and played with freedom. On the ball they expressed themselves, never fearing mistakes. Off the ball they worked hard to win it back.

They got something out of every single game they played in. If the game was too easy, it gave them a chance to have a go at that new skill or try out their weak foot. If it was really tough, then they learned what worked against good players and what didn't.

And always, no matter what, they gave everything that they had so they could leave the pitch with no regrets. Sure, they made mistakes but that's just part of football. That's how they learned. And that's how they still learn, because no footballer is perfect. The best footballers reflect on their performances after a game and see the areas they can improve in. And when success finally does come, they make sure they enjoy it with their team-mates.

## TOP TEN TIPS TO PLAY SMART:

1. Improving as a young footballer is more important than winning. Use games as a chance to try new things and be ready to win when you're older.

2. Mistakes happen. Take risks and if they don't come off, you can learn from them.

3. "P" often: **p**roper **pr**eparation **p**revents **p**oor **p**erformance.

4. Show your strengths. Hide your weaknesses (but train hard to improve them) until they're no longer weaknesses.

5. Enjoy attacking. Enjoy defending. Have fun!

6. Play in lots of different positions in training and matches.

7. Turn anxiety into excitement.

8. Trust your team-mates and help them (even if you're on the bench!).

9. Scan, scan, scan. And remember: awareness › anticipation › action.

10. Believe you're the best player on the pitch (even if you're not!).

# ULTIMATE CHALLENGES TO PLAY SMART:

1. Before each game, list your main strengths and how you are going to use them. Then list the opponents' weaknesses and how you're going to exploit them. Afterwards, reflect on what you did well and what strategies you could improve for the next game.

2. Learn to play in one new position by the end of the season. It doesn't matter if you aren't as good in your new position – you'll learn lots from the experience!

3. Ask to play in a team that is at least one age group above you so that you play against bigger and stronger players. After each game, write down what you learned and the changes you had to make.

4. Open your mouth! Stay in constant communication with the players around you by giving at least five positive instructions in each game. Eventually, communication on the pitch will come naturally to you (and your team-mates will thank you for it!).

5. Check your left shoulder. Check your right shoulder. Check again. Keep checking. Attempt to check your surroundings at least three times every minute. At first it may feel strange, but as you become more confident, try and check even more regularly.

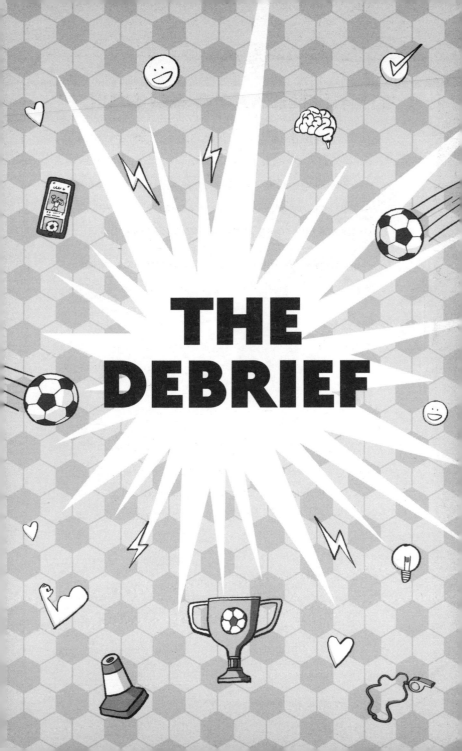

# THE
# DEBRIEF

# QUIZ TIME

What does success look like?

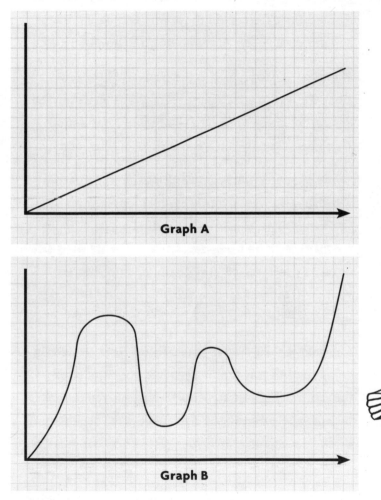

**Graph A**

**Graph B**

Which one did you pick?

The answer is Graph B. Success isn't a straight line. All footballers have setbacks along the way. They lose games, struggle to master skills and have frustrating injuries. The difference in those who end up successful and those who don't all comes down to how they react.

The tricks you've learned in this book will help you along the way to your own success. We've given you the advice, but now it's down to you to put it into action. That's because only you are in control of your journey.

Plenty of people will help you along the way. Coaches will give you advice and friends will support you. Listen to them. You never know what might be useful. Their feedback could help you develop an incredible new skill or turn a weakness into a strength. And don't forget your own feedback loop, which you should continue to use every time you step onto a pitch.

Control the things within your control. Seek challenges. Enjoy yourself. Play football because you want to play football, not because somebody else tells you to. Train because you want to get better. Believe in your ability. Learn from others. Watch your heroes do what they do.

Then put it into action by practising with purpose – even if you do end up being the best player in the entire world. In the words of Belgian attacker **Eden Hazard**:

"If you want to be a top player, you can never be satisfied. You must always want more."

Every day is a chance to learn something new.

Every time you touch the ball, you get better.

Not everyone can become the next **Cristiano Ronaldo** or **Lionel Messi** or **Megan Rapinoe**. But nobody can ever know just how good they could be in the future.

Isn't that exciting?

It's sure to be some football journey. So, lace up your boots, grab a ball and enjoy the ride. Soon enough you'll be playing smarter than ever before.

## TRAIN SMART,
## THINK SMART,
## LIVE SMART,
## PLAY SMART!

# ACKNOWLEDGEMENTS

For a long time we visualized this book coming into being, but without our support network none of this would have been possible.

Our super agent Nick Walters helped take our initial idea and turn it into something so much more. Daisy Jellicoe then took control and gave us some great feedback, which gave us confidence in what we were writing. After that, Charlie Wilson helped to get us over the line.

Many of the ideas that you've read about come from all of the coaches over the years who have believed in us and helped us to be better. For Seth, these coaches include Charlie Brewster, Guy Walton, Kristian Heames, Michael Skubala and Idafe Pérez Jiménez. Matt's inspirational influences include his brilliant brother Tom and the mighty Thundering Typhoons.

Then there's our friends and family who have cheered us on from the sidelines every step of the way.

Finally, there's you: the reader. Thank you for picking up this book. We hope you've enjoyed it.